CONSTELLATIONS

Like the future itself, the imaginative possibilities of science fiction are limitless. And the very development of cinema is inextricably linked to the genre, which, from the earliest depictions of space travel and the robots of silent cinema to the immersive 3D wonders of contemporary blockbusters, has continually pushed at the boundaries. **Constellations** provides a unique opportunity for writers to share their passion for science fiction cinema in a book-length format, each title devoted to a significant film from the genre. Writers place their chosen film in a variety of contexts – generic, institutional, social, historical – enabling **Constellations** to map the terrain of science fiction cinema from the past to the present... and the future.

'This stunning, sharp series of books fills a real need for authoritative, compact studies of key science fiction films. Written in a direct and accessible style by some of the top critics in the field, brilliantly designed, lavishly illustrated and set in a very modern typeface that really shows off the text to best advantage, the volumes in the **Constellations** series promise to set the standard for SF film studies in the 21st century.'
Wheeler Winston Dixon, Ryan Professor of Film Studies, University of Nebraska

 Constellations

Constelbooks

Also available in this series

12 Monkeys Susanne Kord

Blade Runner Sean Redmond

Children of Men Dan Dinello

Close Encounters of the Third Kind Jon Towlson

The Damned Nick Riddle

Dune Christian McCrea

Inception David Carter

RoboCop Omar Ahmed

Rollerball Andrew Nette

Forthcoming

Brainstorm Joseph Maddrey

Ex Machina Joshua Grimm

Jurassic Park Paul Bulloch

Stalker Jon Hoel

CONSTELLATIONS

Mad Max

Martyn Conterio

Acknowledgements

Thanks to Constellations editor John Atkinson, Alexandra Heller-Nicholas, David Eggby, Brian Trenchard-Smith, Lindsay Hallam, Anton Bitel, James Hoare, Adam Lowes, Brendon Connolly, Rebecca Nicole Williams (The Celluloid Sorceress), Dan and Dominique Angeloro (Soda_Jerk) and Lorraine Conterio.

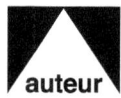

First published in 2019 by
Auteur, 24 Hartwell Crescent, Leighton Buzzard LU7 1NP
www.auteur.co.uk
Copyright © Auteur 2019

Series design: Nikki Hamlett at Cassels Design
Set by Cassels Design www.casselsdesign.co.uk

All rights reserved. No part of this publication may be reproduced in any material form (including photocopying or storing in any medium by electronic means and whether or not transiently or incidentally to some other use of this publication) without the permission of the copyright owner.

British Library Cataloguing-in-Publication Data
A catalogue record for this book is available from the British Library

ISBN paperback: 978-1-911325-86-4
ISBN ebook: 978-1-911325-87-1

Contents

PREFACE: A FEW YEARS FROM NOW 7

INTRODUCTION: BASE BUT SEE IT 9

CHAPTER ONE: GIVE 'EM BACK THEIR HEROES 15

CHAPTER TWO: METAL DAMAGE, BRAIN DAMAGE 31

CHAPTER THREE: THE WHITE LINE NIGHTMARE 55

CHAPTER FOUR: BEYOND ANARCHIE ROAD 77

CONCLUSION 95

BIBLIOGRAPHY 96

PREFACE: A FEW YEARS FROM NOW

Before we deep dive into the nightmare world of *Mad Max* (1979) and the tragic destiny of Max Rockatansky, we must acknowledge, however briefly, Australia's nightmare past. *Mad Max* does not exist solely in a fantasy context or vacuum. Setting the film in a dystopian future was a decision made for several reasons, both creative and financial, which will be discussed later, but it boasted unexpected and profound thematic repercussions. The absence of First Australian communities and characters in the *Mad Max* films becomes more and more striking as the series goes on, as it ventures away from a coastal region and heads into the Outback, reasserting the space as *terra nullius* (nobody's land).

In her July 2017 review of *The Beguiled*, Sofia Coppola's remake of the 1971 gothic melodrama starring Clint Eastwood, Angelica Jade Bastién considered the removal of an African American character from the original film and the novel on which it is based, and described how this absence can actually provide presence. The writer notes 'blackness and racism in general can never be fully removed from stories set in the South, even if black characters themselves are not present. I was struck by how often the absence of black characters felt like a commentary in and of itself, and how distinctly this absence could be felt.'

The first *Mad Max*, ostensibly a revenge yarn about a young man going 'mad' after losing everything, can be read as a cautionary tale in the best sci-fi tradition: how our handling of technology will lead us, not to a new era of enlightenment, but societal decay and our eventual destruction. In the film, we see the end days of Australia's Europeanised settler society, as it teeters on the brink of total collapse, cities and towns plagued by marauding degenerates, the last vestiges of law and order engaged in futile attempts to maintain a semblance of control. The world will soon change. But for First Australians, the world changed centuries ago. Since 1788, when British ships landed at Sydney Cove, First Australians have endured over 200 massacres, marginalisation and suppression of their heritage and culture. George Miller's use of 'A few years from now' points to *Mad Max* and its sequels existing post-genocide.

In *Mad Max: Fury Road* (2015), Miller finally acknowledged First Australians in the *Mad Max* franchise (in the past tense). During one of Max's mental freak-outs, we see a First Australian man (Crusoe Kurddal), credited as The Accusing Dead, appearing in close-up, like a tormented ghost, with bloodshot eyes. Kurddal's appearance is a split-second image in a two-hour action spectacular, but it's there and important as an acknowledgement.

Throughout the series, the director was undoubtedly inspired by aspects of First Australian culture, in numerous ways, from the boomerang in *Mad Max 2* (1982), seeking permission from tribal Elders to film on their land in *Mad Max Beyond Thunderdome* (1985), to his increased interest in First Australian mythologies and storytelling traditions. In 1997, Miller produced for the British Film Institute a documentary, *40,000 Years of Dreaming* (known in Australia as *White Fellas Dreaming: A Century of Australian Cinema*). In it, the director draws parallels between the movies and The Dreaming traditions of First Australian culture, noting specifically, that when he was telling tribal Elders about his plans for *Beyond Thunderdome*, they responded they had heard this story of a hero before. Miller was taken aback, more and more convinced of his 'cinema as mythology' theory and continuum of storytelling in world culture: 'Here were the custodians of a culture 40,000 years old and they were recognising some of their own mythology.'

It is impossible to watch the *Mad Max* series today and not wonder about the lack of First Australians or what can be perceived as their terrible fate 'a few years from now'. I therefore wish to acknowledge Australia's Traditional Owners. I recognise their continuing connection to land, waters and culture. I pay my respects to their Elders past, present and emerging.

INTRODUCTION: BASE BUT SEE IT

George Miller and Byron Kennedy premiered *Mad Max* at Melbourne's East End 1 cinema, on 12 April 1979. Their debut feature film recouped a ballpark AU$350,000-400,000 budget in a matter of days. Within three years, it achieved a staggering worldwide haul somewhere between $100-$150 million. Village Roadshow released the film in Australia, Warner Bros. purchased international distribution rights for 43 countries (one week after its opening in Melbourne, for $1.5 million), while Samuel Z. Arkoff's American International Pictures picked the film up for the US market.

An aesthetic tour de force, *Mad Max*'s symphonic displays of car carnage and autocide is still capable of wowing audiences. As a technological marriage between man and machine, the chase sequences realised Dziga Vertov's 'dream of an anti-humanist cinema of machines in motion. A cinema of conspicuous destruction'. This observation is from director Thom Andersen's *Los Angeles Plays Itself* (2003), as a comment on 1974's American B-movie, *Gone in Sixty Seconds* (and the muscle car movie subgenre in general). It's easily applicable to *Mad Max*. Maybe more so.

Screen entertainment as heavy metal barrage, which if released in Smell-O-Vision would perfume the auditorium with a pungent combo of petrol fumes and sweaty leathers, the movie's unstoppable global success rankled fuddy-duddy newspaper hacks and conservative cultural commentators. For them, the Australian New Wave meant a certain type of prestige picture, the kind shown at film festivals around the world and lauded as art. Miller and Kennedy, a pair of upstarts based in Melbourne, had given Hollywood a run for its money. Put simply, nobody dared make a movie like it in Australia until somebody did. Mark Cousins, in his cinema history book, *The Story of Film*, suggested Miller's directorial brio brought 'an exuberance to Australian filmmaking' (Cousins, 2004: 445). He's not wrong. George Miller's energetic storytelling was atypical of Aussie cinema.

Co-written with James McCausland, who like Mel Gibson was an American living Down Under, he got roped into helping craft cinema history after meeting Miller at a party or down the pub (there are conflicting accounts, though a newspaper interview dated 18 April 1979 mentions Miller met McCausland in a pub). Both were movie buffs and got along well. Miller was especially interested in McCausland's outsider perspective on his homeland. Like with Canadian director Ted Kotcheff's masterpiece on the theme of what today we call 'toxic masculinity', *Wake in Fright* (1971), the outsider's eye can pick up on national character traits and perspectives the natives might not be aware of. Later, the burgeoning filmmaker called up the journalist (McCausland was finance editor at The Australian) and asked if he'd be interested in co-authoring a screenplay. Mainly involved in writing the film's memorable dialogue, while Miller concentrated on the visual aspects, his methodical, mathematical brain mulling over how best to put the pictures in his head up on the screen, the screenplay was written in shot form, almost like a shooting script, and penned at night, as both had day jobs.

Mad Max is a freak picture with a fetish for fast-moving machines and the white-knuckle buzz of action cinema. It's also a dystopian narrative set one second before the great apocalyptic kaboom. Add to this: a revenge tragedy, a muscle car movie, a Western on wheels and a horror film deriving palpable gothic moods from its decayed vision of the world, set amidst haunting landscapes. In press interviews at the time, Miller specifically talked up *Mad Max* as a horror film. He told journalist Vic Caruso, in a Melbourne newspaper interview piece published 18 April 1979: 'It's a horror movie that puts people on the edge of their seats. If you make a horror movie, you simply make people scared. Films only work on the emotions, not on the intellectual process.'

Miller realistically transformed highways and country lanes into arenas of combat and brutal death. Bikers duke it out with a band of cops known as the Main Force Patrol. Toecutter's nomadic criminal gang often appear on screen as if a pack of howling wraiths have manifested and arisen corporally from the two-lane blacktop. There is nothing supernatural at all in *Mad Max*, but Toecutter and his crew have a habit of showing up out of the blue to terrorise and run amok. Their mission is a classic one: to wreak havoc on society and act as they like. The biker-baddies symbolise murder, mayhem, destruction, lawlessness and anti-authoritarian living. Toecutter would no doubt concur with his spiritual 1950s brethren, as well as Peter Fonda's rebellious cri de cœur in *The Wild Angels* (1966): 'We wanna be free! We wanna be free to do what we wanna do. We wanna be free to ride our machines without being hassled by The Man! And we wanna get loaded. And we wanna have a good time. And that's what we're gonna do.' For the Main Force Patrol and the inhabitants of the locations the gang invade and intimidate, Toecutter arriving on the scene is bad news.

Unlike the sequels, the original unfolds in recognisable urban and semi-urban locales: the edges of a city (Melbourne), the countryside and other outskirt environments such as beaches, forests, rural hideaways, cabaret bars, farmsteads, truck stop diners, seaside villages. While such environs are commonplace, at the time of release Australian spaces were something new to international audiences. The land and its people once provided little more than an exotic backdrop for occasional foreign melodramas (such as Alfred Hitchcock's *Under Capricorn*, 1949), but things did change during the 1970s, due to the emergence of the Australian New Wave.

Melbourne in Mad Max. The next city shots in the series occur in Mad Mad Beyond Thunderdome, depicting Sydney after the nuclear holocaust.

We even see Miller use an establishing shot of downtown Melbourne (from afar through the haze of the day). Dotted throughout the film are shots of ferries at sea, planes in the sky, oil derricks pumping the guzzaline (ka-chunk, ka-chunk, ka-chunk), ports, railway lines, harbours and factories. For a movie series so associated with the desolate Outback, the urban-ness of *Mad Max* sets it well apart from the others in the series, all of which ventured further and further into the awe-inspiring and formidable interior of the country, a land which provided a sanctuary-type wilderness for survivors of a nuclear war and its radioactive fallout. We don't see a cityscape again until *Mad Max Beyond Thunderdome* (1985), which eerily depicts Sydney consumed, rusted and ruined by post-fallout gloom.

Mad Max displays an astonishing unity between character, narrative, theme and environment. For liminality binds the film thematically, narratively and environmentally. A hero figure is in transition, society is in transition and the land is in transition. In *Mad Max*, the world might be on the cusp of the gravest catastrophe, but we see people still going about their lives. The daily grind to put food on the table is still a priority, the mundane drudgery of western consumerist living has yet to be transformed wholly into the post-apocalyptic fantastical. It's a long way yet from the dog-eat-dog survival of *Mad Max 2* (1981), the neo-medieval enclave Bartertown in *Mad Max Beyond Thunderdome* or tyrant-king Immortan Joe's Citadel in *Mad Max: Fury Road*.

Upon release, *Mad Max* had its fair share of detractors and fans. It proved to be a film where opinions were strong, for or against. Those who didn't like Miller's sci-fi actioner claimed the film lacked depth, it was nothing but empty spectacle, all style and no substance, an American wannabe rip-off. In postmodernist art, style *is* the substance. *Mad Max*'s great electric beauty is found in the pop art, comic-book effect produced on the screen. Yet often these naysayers, who savaged it in newspapers and magazines, would also grudgingly admit the film was impressive in terms of its technical prowess. To demonstrate the peculiarities in response to *Mad Max*, a 1984 Victoria television guide advertising a showing on Channel 10 (20.30 p.m., on October 11) led with the wonderfully mealy-mouthed quote: 'Base but see it' (1984: 16).

Genre snobbery has long clouded and plagued criticism and reviewing, and it's no different in the reaction to *Mad Max*. Instead of appreciating the film, the lead-in quote basically tells us genre movies struggle for respect. Such thinking in film writing edges towards the hairbrained, but hugely popular concept, known as 'the guilty pleasure'; a mode of thought which often says more about the reviewer than the film itself. The writer continued: 'The film is well made and looks more expensive than it was. The director, George Miller, sustains a mood in his invented world and the film has integrity in that it is unlike anything else that has been made in this country' (ibid.). Elsewhere, Martha DuBose, writing for the Sydney Morning Herald (7 July 1979), described the film as 'so consistently superficial that one cannot excuse its appeal by ascribing to it higher motives or themes.' Critics complained, but the audience wasn't listening. *Mad Max* shifted a whopping 1,447,491 tickets in its homeland. A report in an Australian newspaper, dated 8 June 1979, described an opening night screening in Sydney, at the State Theatre: 'The opening night audience catcalled and threw paper planes when the feature film started late. But after 90 minutes of spine-tingling suspense, they were spellbound. No whistles, no stamping or catcalling – only applause.'

As stated, grindhouse and drive-in specialists AIP oversaw distribution in America (the last foreign title it would import). Talking to TV Week (July 1979), Kennedy explained the deal he'd made with the American distributors: 'They want to release it nationwide – not just in a few cities in, say, Texas, to see how it goes – so that means about 700 prints going out.' He also divulged details of the release campaign: 'At the moment Max looks like opening in the hardtop theatres in February next year [1980], running through the height of the American summer, then being re-launched in the drive-ins.'

Mad Max netted a modest $8 million in rentals. Released stateside during the spring of 1980 to 700 screens (in New York City *Mad Max* ran in 54 theatres), backed by a $2 million advertising budget and roughly $1 million spent on creating hundreds of 35mm prints, *Mad Max* did not perform to the same levels as its popular sequel, released in 1982 as *The Road Warrior*. Warner Bros. disregarded the official title, *Mad Max 2*, for fear it would put American viewers off. *Mad Max* wasn't an outright flop, it made a tidy return, though not the spectacular riches AIP or Miller expected. America wasn't quite ready yet for Max Rockatansky.

Between purchase and release, AIP was sold to Filmways, which decided the Australian voices and colloquialisms were problematic (though AIP had a long tradition of importing foreign titles, then re-cutting and redubbing them, such as Mario Bava's work, starting with 1960's *Black Sunday*). Executives worried Americans wouldn't understand the accents or slang-filled dialogue. It's not unlike the fate of Danny Boyle's *Trainspotting* (1996), released in the US with subtitles, because the Scottish voices were so thick the viewer would struggle to understand the dialogue and dialects. The decision was taken to redub the film with American voices. Yes, that includes Peekskill, New York native Mel Gibson. The actor related to Graham Norton on the popular BBC talk show, The Graham Norton Show, aired in November 2017, how he quickly adapted to his adopted homeland by listening to Barry Humphries records. Curiously, the US dub track appeared in cinemas in the UK, despite the country's history and familiarity with Australia, its accents and culture. Upon re-release in the UK, on VHS tape in 1992, the cover art included a black banner in the top right corner boasting in white lettering 'Features Original Australian Dialogue'. In 2000, US audiences got to hear the original dialogue track, thanks to a limited theatrical re-release by MGM and the following DVD.

Miller hated the US release version most of all because it got rid of Hugh Keays-Byrne's distinct tones and ruined his performance as Toecutter. What's more, it totally erased the distinct Australian-ness of the dialogue and characters, essentially turning the film into what critics originally accused it of being – an American knock-off or wannabe. George Miller is adamant he did not set out to mimic Hollywood or American exploitation cinema, therefore redubbing the dialogue represented an act of cultural vandalism. In Locating Voice in Film (2016), the film's director describes it as 'a genuine Australian film with an international theme.' (2016, 146) Previously, Aussie titles *The Cars That Ate Paris* (1974) and *Patrick* (1978) had been redubbed for their US releases.

The dubbed version is available on the *Mad Max* DVD and is torturous to sit through, but it's there and readily available for anybody feeling brave enough (or is that masochistic?). If you'd like a brief taster and not dine on the whole course, the original AIP trailer has been uploaded to YouTube. The trailer doesn't make enough of the black V8 Interceptor, which might have attracted more petrolheads and it's full of cheesy asides from the trailer's narrator: 'You don't want to make Max mad!'; 'The only law will be a renegade squad of suicidal cops!' The American trailer includes, too, its own colloquialism for hoons ('glory-roaders'), a play on Max's observation to Jess, post-Nightrider chase, when he observes the antagonist was 'just another glory rider, I guess'.

CHAPTER ONE: GIVE 'EM BACK THEIR HEROES

When George Met Bryon

George Miller (born 3 March 1945) became acquainted with Byron Kennedy (born 18 August 1949, died 17 July 1983) at a University of Melbourne film seminar and workshop. Miller had to blag his way onto the course, as technically the prize which led to a seat on the course was won by his brother, Chris, who'd put together a short (the brief was to make a film no longer than 60 seconds), and it earned top spot. George was involved, but not as director.

By the age of 20, Kennedy was working on the periphery of the industry. In his tragically short life, he left a mark as Australia's wunderkind producer. Kennedy was movie-mad from being a kid and always knew that's where his future lay. Miller loved the cinema, but he didn't see it as providing a viable career option, so he chose to study medicine. Right up until *Mad Max*'s production, he was working as a locum doctor, Kennedy serving as his driver.

At 18, Kennedy founded Warlok Films. A couple of years later, he'd directed an award-winning short documentary (*Hobson's Bay*, recipient of the Kodak Trophy in 1969) and found employment making industrial films. He occasionally lectured at an experimental Melbourne film school and worked as a freelance cameraperson. His go-getter attitude and gift of the gab made him the perfect foil to the quieter Miller. In terms of *Mad Max*'s evolution, it is Kennedy who was the petrolhead, the car obsessive. He loved technology and anything to do with speed. The V8 black-on-black Interceptor represented Kennedy's idea of the dream automobile. Kennedy keenly oversaw the modifications made to the XB Falcon, his creative input helping craft what is one of the most iconic vehicles in cinema history.

Friends and artistic collaborators, Kennedy and Miller experienced success for the first time in 1971, when the satirical short they'd made, *Violence in the Cinema, Part 1*, was deemed so good, it was picked up for distribution in Australia and Britain. Shown before a programmed feature, back in the day when film schedules often included shorts and B pictures, *Violence in the Cinema, Part 1* was a major win in their journey towards *Mad Max*. In 1973, Kennedy received a grant from the Film and Television School, to learn about producing and financing. He visited Europe, Asia and Los Angeles. Kennedy and Miller also worked together on *The Devil in Evening Dress* (1974), a television special investigating the ghost of an opera singer said to haunt Melbourne's Princess Theatre. By 1975, Kennedy and Miller finally began to cook up an idea for a feature film. After further trips abroad for Kennedy, including the Cannes Film Festival market and several more visits to Hollywood, learning about such things as contracts, their project cranked up a notch.

The Result of an Anxiety

'Perhaps it's the result of an anxiety?' says bleach-blonde baddie, Bubba Zanetti (Geoff Parry), Toecutter's second-in-command, in response to a query from a young lad (Brendan Young) about a totalled car sitting in the courtyard at the Halls of Justice. 'Looks like it was chewed up and spat out,' the boy comments. *Mad Max* was the result of an anxiety. Several, in fact.

Australians love their cars. While the car-manufacturing industry in the country is dead as a dodo, car and racing culture is alive and kicking (including a subculture involving illegal engine modifications). The passion for automobiles began proper in the 1950s and gripped like a vice. In *Mad Max: Fury Road*, Miller reflected on his country's history with the automobile by creating a new religion from it. The worship of cars is the ultimate nightmare evolution of Australia's love affair with motoring and speed. In the post-apocalyptic wasteland, the War Boys pray to the V8 engine (the nitro-charged engine serving as the beating heart of the black-on-black Interceptor) and they are prepared to sacrifice their lives and die in a blaze of glory, if asked to by their warlord leader, Immortan Joe (Hugh Keays-Byrne). Valhalla awaits them... or so they believe. In the film, worshippers make a holy sign with joined hands, interlocked fingers mimicking the cylinders protruding from the body of the engine. Steering wheels, too, serve as holy-like relics as much as bits of personalised, branded kit. The origin or kernel of the idea for this might well be the rain-and-mud bacchanal montage sequence in *Mad Max 2*, where Lord Humungus' clan attempt to intimidate the compound dwellers with displays of aggression involving their bikes and cars. The scene is like a primal ritual or war-dance involving man and machine.

In *Mad Max: Fury Road*, technology addiction and automobile fetishism has triumphed and reached an apotheosis in its elevation to spiritual realms. Cars, Christianity, Norse mythology and Buddhist reincarnation have been co-opted from memories of the old world into a new form. 'I live, I die, I live again!' War Boy, Nux (Nicholas Hoult) exclaims, showcasing his narrow and deluded outlook. Fury Road is a state of mind as much as it is a designated stretch of desert. The root of this journey to religion began with *Mad Max*'s focus on 'hoon' culture, the rise in road fatalities in the 1970s and a vision of the near future which sees the law prepared to play as down and dirty as the crooks they're supposed to bring to book.

Cars and motorbikes represent a literal and symbolic avenue to freedom and escape from stifling home lives. It is a cultural bridge between America and Australia. They share gigantic landscapes, big skies and roads that seem endless. Getting your first set of wheels is a rite of passage into adulthood. Tear-arsing around, intimidating locals, acting rebellious, burning rubber, these pastimes are exclusively associated with males and serve as displays of masculine behaviour. Ken Hannam's New Wave classic, *Sunday Too Far Away* (1975), is a great example of the recklessness of the Australian male driver. The film begins with Jack Thompson's bushman falling asleep at the wheel and crashing his car. It rolls and rolls, until left as a twisted wreck covered in Outback dust. He gets out, checks himself and walks off unscathed but also unconcerned. *Sunday Too Far Away* and other films present the wrecked car set against the Australian landscape as something quintessentially related to the country. The coining of the word 'hoon', an Australian term of murky origin, denotes a person who drives fast and recklessly. Hoon behaviour is key to *Mad Max*'s connecting specifically with Aussie audiences. Australia's open expanses practically invite speed junkies to put pedal to the metal. In more recent times, Australian legislation has been applied to cover the open waves. Jet skis have become an issue.

The first iteration of *Mad Max* did not involve a cops-and-robbers setup. Nor the bleak dystopian future setting or car chases. Max Rockatansky was a journalist who followed car crashes and interviewed people and victims involved. The problem Kennedy and Miller faced was making their idea work as a movie. Where was the connecting drama? The narrative propulsion? As a topic, it certainly held contemporary resonance, as well as carrying a vaguely JG Ballard-style influence, but how to dramatise the car wrecks? In a moment of inspiration, Max switched professions from newshound to beleaguered police officer. The next creative step was arguably the most important. Each film takes us further and further into a world gone nuts. *Mad Max 2* unfolds in the Outback, set on dusty asphalt roadways and among starkly rocky hills (filming took place in Broken Hill, New South Wales). *Mad Max Beyond Thunderdome* went for a desert look, with Coober Pedy chosen for its barren, sandy vistas. *Mad Max: Fury Road* is even bleaker, with gnarled Namibian mountains resembling giant cancerous tumours; the land is diseased.

Regarding *Mad Max*, pushing the film's narrative into a near-future Australia where society is collapsing, not only minimised the cultural cringe factor, it implanted an inherent sense of dread to proceedings. With a miniscule budget, Miller also needed to select locations which were affordable. Economic considerations forced him into choosing environments which looked defunct and dirty. Production designers could enhance the decrepit quality already there. As the story was heightened from the norm, a futuristic setting seemed apt. *Mad Max* was now a science-fiction saga.

In Miller's vision of a country going down the swanny, the distinction between the hoon and the cop was deliberately blurred (Miller filmed but excised a short scene featuring Max and Goose drag-racing in their official police vehicles). Max understands the thin blue line between hero and villain, creating a self-awareness in a character far different from other maverick coppers of the 1970s screen, who would recoil at the suggestion their hard-line tactics and distain for bureaucrats made them borderline wrong 'uns. Max tells commanding officer, Fifi (Roger Ward), 'It's that rat circus out there. I'm beginning to enjoy it.' He further adds: 'Any longer out on that road and I'm one of them, you know? A terminal crazy. Only I got a bronze badge to say I'm one of the good guys.'

Another vital aspect in the construction of the film's dystopian vision was the director's medical background and years working as a doctor, as well as his exposure to road accidents growing up, which were frequent enough to leave a lasting mark. During his stint as a doctor, he saw plenty of human roadkill and mangled bodies wrought from car crashes. 'Metal damage, brain damage,' as Vincent Gil's memorable psychotic, The Nightrider, poetically puts it to the Bronze (the nickname given to the Main Force Patrol, by the villains). Miller's medical background also led him to name Max Rockatansky in honour of nineteenth-century pathologist, Carl von Rokitansky.

When it comes to injury detail and the staging of accidents, there exists in *Mad Max* a tendency towards realism; the approach to the results of great violence is far from mindless. Critics read the movie as cynical and exploitative of its subject matter, but a cautionary, moralistic underpinning can be gleaned. Doctor Miller shows the audience what happens when flesh and machines tangle. It isn't pretty. The director explained how his medical background, years growing up in Queensland and witnessing accidents on the lanes inspired him: 'It somehow resonated with me because I remember the feeling of working in casualty at St. Vincent's Hospital and being quite disturbed by the violence, and the road carnage, and the way we kind of processed it,' the director recalled. Talking to Cinema Papers, in 1979, Miller mentioned how, in his youth, he'd lost several pals: 'I grew up in a country town in Queensland where I saw a lot of road accidents. There was definitely a subculture surrounding cars and violence, and I lost three friends in accidents, when they were teenagers.'

Without straight up sermonising on the perils of fast-driving, Miller peppered his film with scenes and dialogue bringing home the horrors of road accidents. During the film's opening chase, Goose (Steve Bisley) is eating lunch at Fat Nancy's truck stop eatery. The bloke sitting opposite him loses his appetite, as the lawman gruesomely relates a smash he witnessed: 'I saw it in slow motion. He leaves the seat and goes through the windscreen, headfirst straight into the tree, right? Then, bounces back through the windscreen, and by the time we got to him, he was just sitting there, trying to scream with his face ripped off.'

Main Force Patrol car unit Big Bopper, driven by the comic duo Charlie (John Lay) and Roop (Steve Millichamp), crash out of the film's opening chase sequence, having careened into a motorhome. Charlie's throat is shredded. He grips torn flesh tightly, blood seeping between the fingers. The windshield of their car is everywhere, some of it sticking into Charlie's throat. The cop leans back in total shock. The framing and shot, too, is one of the few instances of handheld camera in the film, heightening the shift to gritty realism. Charlie ends up losing his voice box and having to communicate with an electronic device, making him sound like a robot.

Another key moment is the aftermath of a chase we never see. Max has been engaged in racing down hoons on the highway. Ambulances, the media, Main Force Patrol officers and scrap-metal trucks dot the night-time scene. There is a close-up of a bloodied man twitching in the driver's seat. 'The old meat grinder's humming tonight, eh?' Fifi comments, surveying the devastation like a four-star general in the field after a battle. Again, this short sequence is set up realistically. The aftermath sequence could be something we see on the evening news or on the motorway, as we rubberneck looking for signs of life-changing physical damage and twisted ruins where once was a car.

Goose's bike crash begins as a scene illustrating the pleasures and joys of speeding on country lanes. After a night of fun with a singer picked up from the Sugartown Cabaret, the always cheerful and upbeat cop heads off back to work. He's going hell for leather down twisting, turning roads, the speedometer clocking max speed. The fact he's an officer of the law means nothing. The setup, however, is classic Hitchcock (specifically his definition of cinematic suspense), which he detailed to François Truffaut, in the French New Wave director's classic interview book. Hitch decided suspense works far better on screen if the audience has more information than the characters. Miller adheres to this belief several times in his film. Hitch's example was a family conversation at the dinner table. An innocuous, even mundane scene is then thrillingly turned on its head as Hitchcock imagined an anarchist, for some reason of political terror or cause, has placed a bomb underneath the table and the family has no idea what is in store. The audience knows there is a bomb underneath the table. They are privy to the info, but the family members oblivious. 'The public is participating in the scene. The audience is longing to warn the characters on the screen' (Truffaut, 1968: 52).

Goose's crash, like the mid-point set-up in the opening chase scene involving three MFP units (Big Bopper, March Hare and Goose) chasing the Nightrider through a country town, is Hitchcock's theory in motion. Here, though, it's played slightly differently. We know Johnny The Boy (Tim Burns) has loosened a few nuts and bolts on the wheels of Goose's bike. The sequence of shots featuring Goose hurtling down the lane produces a sense of exhilaration in the viewer, maybe something akin to euphoria, but a cruel suspense is formed too. The low-angled establishing wide shots of the bike riding, shots of the wheels and POV-style images noting the maximum speed at which the bike is burning rubber, deliver a rollercoaster effect. Brian May's bombastic orchestral music screams and the loud revving noise from the bike's engine screams to us louder: something bad is about to happen to Goose!

The bike begins to shake, Goose is thrown off into the tall grass (stunt coordinator, Grant Page, performed the stunt). But even here, Miller is toying with our expectations, as Goose survives the crash relatively unscathed. It's a second wave attack, after he's driving a tow truck away from the initial accident, where the Goose is finally cooked. An awaiting Johnny the Boy throws a hub cap through the windshield, causing the vehicle to roll down an embankment. Upside down, trapped, engine oil and fuel leaking over him, poor Jim is burned alive by a visibly hesitant Johnny. The scene in which the pig is roasted serves as an act of fealty to the king (Toecutter). 'Light me, Johnny,' the Big Bad asks. As a scene of depravity and brutality against an officer of the law, the murder of Goose was likely to shock conservative sensibilities and lead to critical backlash, but the scene is pivotal to the film's narrative, as it fuels Max's eventual outburst and revenge plot. There is a poetic, though macabre, justice and symbolism to the film's finale, too. Johnny the Boy goes up in flames, in reprisal of Goose's death in almost the exact manner. Fire purges Max's anger, leaving behind the burned-out shell of a man.

Later, at the hospital, Max approaches his mate apprehensively, a UV light shining in the centre of the bed. Poor Goose is completely cloaked to protect his burnt flesh from infection. Then, as in a traditional horror movie, Miller delivers a jump scare: Goose's blackened arm falls out of the bed. Max moves closer and closer, pulling away the bedsheet. We don't see Goose burnt to a cinder. The film's low budget forced Miller into letting our imaginations run wild. Instead, he used a special effect to register Max's reaction. The frame ripples, as if an image writ in water. The moment is like a terrible dream or a cinematic recreation of the emotion which hits us upon tragic news. We feel unsteady, punched in the gut, at a complete loss. The unstable image mirrors the emotion and disbelief in his eyes. It's the type of sudden reaction Miller would have seen etched on the faces of patients and their families during his time as a doctor.

Finally, in the book *Miller and Max*, the director specifically remembered one victim of a car crash. She had bloody stumps where her legs should have been. It is hard not to think of this detail as directly influencing the fate of Max's wife Jess, played by Joanna Samuel, when she lies in the intensive care unit in hospital, visited by a distraught Max, an arm and leg amputated. Doctor George must have seen all kinds of unpleasantness in his days as an A&E professional, but how he dealt and processed this in his debut film is psychologically and creatively fascinating.

It's the Oil, Stupid!

1970s Australia was beset by economic woes, environmental disasters and political change. The country's involvement in the Vietnam war finally ended in 1973, with the loss of thousands of lives, leaving citizens, like folk in the United States, wondering what was the purpose and benefit of the bloody venture? Communism wasn't vanquished, it had defeated the world's number one superpower. The pervading mood of *Mad Max* is Australia decaying, going wrong, heading towards calamity, losing its way fast. All Miller and McCausland had to do was frame these social and political conditions in the context of a genre flick.

The 1973 oil crisis was a specific influence on the film. To McCausland and Miller, it revealed an ugly side to humanity and panic culture in western countries. The oil wars had been building since the late 1960s, with the 1973 crisis a culmination of geo-political strife stemming from the Middle East and business relations between it and western nations. It was a direct retaliation against the USA, its foreign policy in the region and military support of Israel during the Yom Kippur war (fought against Egypt). Middle Eastern OPEC countries (Organisation of Petroleum Exporting Countries) slowed production and imposed export trade embargoes to the USA and others heavily dependent on foreign oil. The cost of oil shot up from $3 to $12 per barrel, forcing petrol prices to rise and bringing fears of rationing. The feuds over oil and the war between Israel and Egypt were felt globally, leading to panic at the pumps.

As a low-budget actioner, Miller had to use an on-screen legend ('A few years from now') and infer troubled times through *mise en scène* and storytelling. As the series developed and received greater budgets, the director could run with the apocalyptic ball. *Mad Max 2* was able to make the implicit explicit, with its clever opening montage made up of newsreels depicting oil derricks, rowdy political meetings and street scenes of anarchic confrontations. The narrative, too, puts the oil crisis up front and centre, as it features a fight between a marauding gang led by the 'Ayatollah of Rock 'n' Rolla', Lord Humungus (Kjell Nilsson), a hulking S&M fetish-wear enthusiast who sports a hockey mask to hide a disfigured face, and a group protecting their prized asset (oil). There was a repeat of the 1973 oil crisis in 1979, upon the Iran Revolution and the subsequent Iran-Iraq war.

Writing for the Courier-Mail (2006), McCausland wrote about how the oil crisis provided the futuristic film's core fundamentals: 'George and I wrote the script based on the thesis that people would do almost anything to keep vehicles moving and the assumption that nations would not consider the huge costs of providing infrastructure for alternative energy until it was too late.'

While the oil shortage has little overall bearing on the movie's narrative (though there is a scene of Toecutter's gang stealing petrol from a truck on a highway), the OPEC crisis helped the pair envision a world pulling itself apart and edging towards anarchy. McCausland further discussed the crisis in Luke Buckmaster's book: 'A couple of oil strikes that hit many pumps revealed the ferocity in which Australians would defend their right to fill a tank. Long queues formed at the stations with petrol–and anyone who tried to sneak ahead in the queue met raw violence.' (Buckmaster, 2017: 27)

Casting *Mad Max*

For years, NIDA (National Institute of Dramatic Arts) graduate Mel Gibson liked to tell a tall story about how he bagged the role of Max Rockatansky. According to him, he was involved in a bar fight the night before accompanying a pal (presumably Steve Bisley) to an audition. All bloodied and bruised, the casting agent took one look and said to him, 'We need freaks like you.' Alas, the truth is more prosaic.

Miller searched high and low, at home and abroad, for his Max. At the time of the fortuitous meeting between the director and the drama grad, Gibson was living in a student house near Bondi Beach, Sydney (one of his room-mates was Bisley). Both came to Miller's attention at the suggestion of a casting agent, who told the director to check out the latest crop of NIDA graduates and maybe he'll find young actors to fill roles. Gibson received AU$15,000 for the gig, though *Mad Max* was not his debut film (that would be 1977's *Summer City*).

In a filmed interview on the Australian Screen website, Miller described meeting Gibson and finally landing his Max:

> I remember Mitch Matthews, the casting agent, said there's a couple of NIDA graduates you should meet. And I remember late one afternoon after screen testing lots and lots of people, Mel Gibson came in and I was very, very exhausted. I remember watching through the video camera lens as he's running this scene and I suddenly started to believe it. And I thought, oh my god, there's something going on here. And halfway through that test he was [snaps fingers] … I was just so grateful he was around.

Any action hero needs a worthy adversary. Having struck gold in landing Gibson as Max, Kennedy and Miller struck gold again when they cast Hugh Keays-Byrne, an English-Australian actor, to play the demented Toecutter. The former Royal Shakespeare Company member took a Method approach to the role and considered Toecutter to be the film's true hero, beautifully aligning with the film's portrait of the disintegrating line between good and bad. He created a great camaraderie on set with the lads cast as his gang members. They became his boys, his army.

Toecutter is an unusual villain. The way he acts with his gang is peculiar, featuring clear hints of homoeroticism, a theme developed in *Mad Max 2*, and a distinct vanity. His movements are unpredictable and eccentric. In one scene, he expresses displeasure with a hiss. Instead of screaming and shouting, Toecutter has a quieter threat about him, an authority which rarely needs flexing to keep others in line. He speaks in whispery tones, his voice somewhere between dripping honey and a mad king about to go apoplectic. In his animal skins and with that unkempt frizzy hairdo, Toecutter looks like a confused bear awoken long before hibernation is over. He is one of the most distinct Big Bads in all of cinema, not just Australian, and Keays-Byrne is a magnetic presence.

The Shoot

There are plenty of movies dotted throughout cinema history labelled troubled productions. Moviemaking is hard work, even more so when money is tight and schedules tighter. *Mad Max* was initially scheduled to be a 10-week shoot. With a great percentage of the film taking place outdoors or using interiors at real locations, along with shooting complex sequences with one camera, there was always going to be stress involved in getting scenes in the can. The 10-week shoot turned into 12. *Mad Max* filmed at locations around Victoria. As well as Melbourne and Geelong, other sites and towns included Wallan, Clunes, Black Rock and Fairhaven. Rolling before the cameras on 24 October 1977, disruptions plagued filming from the start and Miller seriously considered firing himself.

The history of the shoot is detailed brilliantly in *Miller and Max* (2017), where all manner of goofs, gaffes and stupidity are related. One good example is the first day of filming, when the location manager hadn't secured permission to shoot on a bridge (the scene where Johnny The Boy makes a call on a highway telephone on an overpass over the Geelong Freeway). Nobody, most importantly not even the guy charged with managing the set, had thought about the logistics of holding up traffic or where the crew would park. Miller and his core team turned up and nothing had been set up. It was all a bit absurd, all a bit amateur hour. Such issues threatened to expose Kennedy and Miller as two creatives hopelessly out of their depth and ill-prepared for turning the written page and images inside George's head into celluloid magic. Everything naysayers had said – that they were out of their element, out of their depth, a pair of crazies who'd get people killed – looked prophetic. During filming, the pair received little in the way of respect from the crew, with much opprobrium and shade thrown at Miller. Kennedy telephoned filmmaker Brian Trenchard-Smith and asked him to fly down from Sydney and direct the film in Miller's place, according to Trenchard-Smith, in a Skype interview conducted for this book. He said he'd kept quiet about this part of *Mad Max* history, out of respect for Miller. Trenchard-Smith was close to the film's production at the time as he was stuntman Grant Page's manager. He'd secured an AU$10,000 fee (3% of the film's budget) for Page. Trenchard-Smith was impressed, too, by the amount of pre-production preparation Miller and Kennedy had undertaken. They'd looked at car chases and had a clear plan for what they wanted to achieve. Trenchard-Smith explained: 'At a certain point, it might have been in the second week of shooting, I got a call from Byron Kennedy and he asked would you come down to Melbourne and co-direct with George? He's having trouble making decisions and we're falling behind and so forth.'

Trenchard-Smith saw that Kennedy was in a difficult position. If the film wasn't finished and the production fell apart, their prospective careers in cinema would be over before they'd properly started. Trenchard-Smith mulled the proposal and decided against it. 'I turned it down because I knew how devastating it could be to someone's career. To be replaced or have someone come in and basically take over control of the directing, on your first film?' The decision partly sprung from personal experience on his own first feature, describing factions working against him and if not for an adamant producer backing him up, he'd have been fired. 'I too was a little slow [getting things together] on the first week of my first movie and it was a bit overwhelming.' The director sided with Miller in the spirit of recognising directing your first feature film, especially one as complicated as *Mad Max*, was bloody hard. 'I didn't want to do that to George. I liked Byron too. I suggested they go get a strong first AD (Assistant Director) and back him [Miller] up. And I think that's what they did.'

Miller can look back on the production of *Mad Max* with amazement that nobody was killed. Being a qualified doctor, he was obsessively concerned with the stunt work and people getting injured. It's understandable enough, since he'd be the one getting sued to the hilt and having to live with himself. In general, Victoria Police cooperated with the production, though they were largely ignorant of the type of movie being made on their streets. Cinematographer David Eggby, interviewed for this book, recalled the stunt work and his involvement in capturing shots while on motorbike: 'The stunts were very dangerous. [There were] no safety rules and regulations, back then. We were all a bit gung-ho. Stupid and young, I guess. I think what made the film so different was everyone, actors, crew, stunts, just went for it. There were a few accidents, stunt co-ordinator Grant Page crashed out on a motorbike broke his leg early on in production. Unfortunately, the original leading lady Rosie Bailey was riding pillion with Grant and she also broke her leg. They quickly recast [the role with] Joanna Samuel. [There were a] few close shaves, like coming face to face with quarry tip trucks refusing to acknowledge our crude attempt at traffic control.'

Not only did the crew not have the required permits or authority to shut down whole sections of highway, sometimes at rush hour, with thousands of cars and people wanting to get to and from work, but what Miller envisioned was bonkers and hadn't been attempted before on such a local level. This grey area led to Kennedy inventing a permit (he told crew it was given to him by an 'Inspector Bloggs'), to be shown to nosey coppers who inquired as to what was going on. This permit gave them permission to film anywhere, at any time. Cast and crew still laugh about it, over 40 years later, referring to it as the 'Get Out of Jail Free' card.

Melbourne University's southern car park doubled for the MFP Halls of Justice garage in Mad Max.

Mad Max was filmed on an Arriflex 35BL, using Todd AO lenses sent down from Hollywood as second-hand kit. David Eggby detailed how the film came to be shot the way it was: 'George Miller and Byron Kennedy wanted the movie shot in a CinemaScope format 2.35:1 ratio and because of budget restrictions were looking at shooting the film in Techniscope, a 2-perf pull frame system used to shoot many old spaghetti westerns. I think the stock cost compared to the normal 4-perf timing was substantial and it automatically gave you a CinemaScope format without cropping. There were a couple of 2-perf cameras available in Melbourne and the lenses were just normal spherical lenses, the problem was the lab. We could get the negative processed but getting a 2-perf print was not available in Australia, then a positive would have to be printed and processed overseas with about a week turnaround.'

When the set of Todd AO anamorphic lenses was discovered, the DoP and director decided they were the best suited to capturing the images in Miller's head. Eggby recalled: 'There was a set of Todd AO anamorphic lenses in Sydney, at one of the rental houses. There weren't many to choose from but enough focal lengths to shoot the movie. They were slow and needed constant recalibration, but they were beautiful bits of glass. In 1977, apart from Panavision, all other systems were a bit of a mixture of add-ons. So eventually I shot *Mad Max* with the Todd AO lenses with an add-on spherical to anamorphic viewfinder, that was so bad I ended up shooting the movie through the original spherical viewfinder. You quickly get used to framing a skiing vertically stretched image. But we had a 4-perf Anamorphic negative that was fantastic.'

After filming wrapped, a prolonged and intensive post-production period began. *Mad Max* took its sweet time getting to the screen, with minor reshoots, inserts, editing and mixing taking up to 10 months. Kennedy and Miller knew the process would take a while and took the decision to edit *Mad Max* on a 16mm work-print (they couldn't afford 35mm editing equipment). This is a dicey approach, as it threatens the negative. British-born Margaret Cardin (who worked as negative cutter/matcher for Peter Weir from *The Cars That Ate Paris* up to *The Year of Living Dangerously* (1982)) was tasked with neg-matching 1700 shots from anamorphic 35mm to the 16mm work-print reduction. This she did virtually by eye. Kennedy later said they would have been lost without Cardin's sterling contribution in post-production. An editor and negative cutter with a fascinating career in British and Australian film, Cardin subsequently made a cameo appearance in *Beyond Thunderdome*.

Editor Tony Patterson beavered away for four months with George Miller, cutting the picture. After this period, Cliff Hayes took over, as Patterson had to leave due to work commitments on the film *Dimboola* (1979). Five months full-time work was also put into the soundtrack and mixing stage. Mixed at Armstrong Studios in Melbourne, the studio's stock in trade was advertising and music, not film post-production. Kennedy told Cinema Papers: 'We knew if we wanted a conventional mix in a conventional mixing studio, we would be there for weeks and weeks. We knew it was going to be extremely complex because we wanted to synthesize a lot of sound–to harmonize tracks by putting them through digital time delays and Marshall Time Modulators. We also wanted to experiment and give the soundtrack much more body–more oomph!' (1979: 368)

In a July 2019 interview, with the American website Indiewire, ostensibly looking back on the production of *Mad Max: Fury Road*, George Miller mentioned to journalist Anne Thompson, that the toughest film he ever directed was his debut. 'I didn't know much about filmmaking, and it was rather bewildering. I was aware of the process. It took me a good 10 years before I could watch that first movie again, because all I would see were the mistakes – the things I felt were left to do creatively.'

CHAPTER TWO: METAL DAMAGE, BRAIN DAMAGE

Mad Max and the New Wave

To quote the elderly narrator in *Mad Max 2*, in order to understand how George Miller came to make his first film and how a resurgent Australian film industry helped *Mad Max* into being, we have to go back to another time... a time when Australian filmmaking was nothing but 'ruined dreams, this wasted land.' For it is here, in this blighted, moribund, barely functioning industry, Australians learned to make films again.

Australian film production was in serious trouble after the Second World War. Even earlier, like other countries after the First World War (1914-1918), it had had to contend with the raging popularity of American movies. Director Ken G. Hall, who turned out commercial fare through his CineSound company in the 1930s, described the post-war period in *The New Australian Cinema* as a 'grim doldrum' (Hall, 1980: 8). Aussie film industry woes in fact precede the world's first global conflict, going as far back as 1910, when distributors and exhibitors merged, shutting out locally made films in favour of foreign titles. It became known as 'the combine' and was dominated by Australian Films and Union Theatres. With no chance of films being seen, what was the point in making them? Producers and directors might as well have burned all their money in a fire pit in the garden. Andrew Pike's essay on the history of the early years in *The New Australian Cinema* described the negative effect on Australian-made pictures:

> Displaying little interest in Australian production, the combine concentrated on filling theatres with imported films, and Australian production companies began to fade within months. In 1911, more than 10 production companies made 50-odd fiction films, but by the end of 1912, only five or six companies were in existence, and only 30 features had been produced that year. In 1913, less than 20 films had appeared, and the number declined even further in the following years. (1980: 11)

From the late 1960s, where film output was virtually zero, to around 20 films a year in the late 1970s, the New Wave was no mad gold rush, but did enough to bear fruit. It became clear filmmakers would adapt well enough in America, where it was relatively easier to get a movie made. A February 1981 New York Times article, by Australian film critic Keith Connolly, discussed how New Wave artistry appeared to be modelled explicitly on (or is that making eyes at?) Hollywood. In *Mad Max*'s case, the accents, customs and milieu might well be different, but the universality of the cinematic syntax, storytelling craft and action is what made it shine and do gangbusters on the international market. But does that make it expressly American in form? Miller denied it, as we know. Yet Connolly saw the New Wave crowd as indebted to American moviemaking. 'While all the best recent Australian films have a distinctive national flavor, most obvious in their rich visual texture, their very acceptability is rooted in a recognizably American format.'

Successive administrations, up until the late 1960s, had been largely deaf to the pleas of producers and directors. Calls for quotas on foreign films and, more importantly, financial assistance in the form of tax breaks had been discussed way, way back in the 1910s. Several half-hearted attempts were made throughout the years, but nothing ever truly stuck until John Gorton's administration established a film bank. Legislation was passed for the creation of the Australian Film and Television Development Corporation (which became the Australian Film Commission). In 1972, the Australian Film and Television School was birthed into existence, along with a funding body for experimental cinema. Phillip Noyce and Gillian Armstrong were among 1973's AFTS intake. Opportunities for directors to make their films was described by Bruce Beresford in the documentary feature, *David Stratton: A Cinematic Life* (2017): 'It was like a whole lot of people crawling across the desert and all of a sudden [there was] somebody with water.'

Until the Gorton action plan, continued by the Whitlam administration (1972-1975), the same old mistakes and reticence to get to grips with the situation had been repeated over and over. It wasn't a question of pumping money into the industry, there were specific issues surrounding Aussie culture. Phillip Adams described the thirty-year period until the 1970s in *The New Australian Cinema* (Murray, 1980), for which he provided the book's foreword, as a time when his country suffered from an inferiority complex (known as 'cultural cringe'). There were more local questions, too, on the theme of Aussie accents. *Mad Max* was dubbed for the American market, and no doubt was dubbed for other foreign markets; where dubbing is a standard convention as much as subtitling, but Adams had a strong point to make regarding his homeland and Australian voices. He noted how people rarely heard an Aussie accent on the stage, on television or radio, unless it was a comedian doing Strine. 'We needed to hear our own accent. We wanted our voice to be heard in the world' (Adams, 1980: 7).

1992 Re-release cover artwork describing its widescreen presentation and the original Australian dialogue soundtrack.

Australian producers regularly bemoaned Hollywood's cultural and financial hegemony. Yet it's no big mystery as to why audiences love American movies, have always loved American movies, will always love American movies and prefer them to local product. Filmmakers buggered off to the States the first chance they got. Peter Weir became one of Hollywood's most prestigious talents, essentially shedding his Aussie background to become a storyteller *sans frontières* and went on to dismiss the tag 'New Wave'. In 1985 he directed *Witness*, a cop thriller and pastoral melodrama (think: Hitchcock meets Murnau), set in Pennsylvania's reclusive Amish community. Starring Harrison Ford, it is one of the most acclaimed Hollywood films of the decade and received Oscars for Best Screenplay and Film Editing. Weir was the first filmmaker of his generation to conquer Hollywood and hasn't made a film back home since 1982's Mel Gibson-starring *The Year of Living Dangerously*. In a February 1981 NY Times article, Weir noted there was no iconoclast 'Australian Godard' among the current raft of directors. He's right. The arthouse side of Australian New Wave would exemplify tastefulness and a middle-class view of drama. There was nothing radical going on in the mainstream (which strengthens Connolly's observation). No Australian director made anything equivalent to Godard's *Breathless* (1960), it's true, but it's arguable Weir's dismissal of the tag is a touch too literal and another example of cultural cringe.

Mad Max and Ozploitation

In the 1969 Arts Council Report, a recommendation was made to start producing genre films for local markets. This is where *Mad Max* looks to fit in, regarding the general scheme of things. It was part of the genre boom, but its stellar success meant it went way beyond the confines of the local market. As noted, whatever the New Wave was, in the minds of cultural gatekeepers it didn't include the likes of *Mad Max* and other genre films. In her 2017 Miskatonic Institute of Horror Studies lecture on Australian genre cinema, Lindsay Hallam discussed this tension between the image of the New Wave and genre output: 'There was also a surge in genre films made in the 1970s, so alongside the arthouse and period drama films were horror films, action films and comedies. While the period films were released to much acclaim, the genre films were heavily criticised and, until recently, almost erased from Australian cinema history' (Hallam, 2017).

'Probably the classiest B-grade trash ever made,' Mel Gibson told Films and Filming journalist Dalya Alberge, in a profile interview of the rising star (1983: 22). Ostensibly referring to *Mad Max 2* (1981), this self-deprecating judgement is easily applicable to the original. A few years before Gibson offered this assessment Byron Kennedy, interviewed for Cinema Papers magazine (May/June 1979), made a similar comment. When asked whether the film he'd produced bore relation to the B-movies of AIP or Roger Corman, he replied: 'No. It's much more up-market than Corman or

AIP films.' He then described the film, echoing Gibson, as 'a highly-sophisticated B-grade film' (1979: 367).

Where does *Mad Max* fit into the landscape of the Australian New Wave of the 1970s? Does it belong at all? Historically it has been lumped in with what became known as Ozploitation, the second-tier genre works which emerged in the decade. At the time of *Mad Max*'s release in April 1979, Australia's national cinema and industry was well into its glorious renaissance. From this fecund era, alongside George Miller and Mel Gibson, directors, actors and cinematographers would emerge such as Peter Weir, Fred Schepisi, Phillip Noyce, Gillian Armstrong, Dean Semler, Judy Davis, John Seale, Russell Boyd and Donald McAlpine. The sea change in Australian cinema's fortunes helped create for the first time what became a furtive and sustained period of film making activity. The films it produced are today considered classics of Australian cinema.

As argued in the introduction, Miller's debut is a misfit movie, a freak among the pack. It's a low-budget genre film that did blockbuster-sized business and boasts an aesthetic finesse and directorial panache which sets it apart from Ozploitation. Nothing like it had been seen in Australia before. *Mad Max* is frequently associated with 'Ozploitation', the term coined in the noughties by Quentin Tarantino as 'Aussieploitation' and shortened by Mark Hartley to Ozploitation, for his excellent documentary, *Not Quite Hollywood: The Wild, Untold Story of Ozploitation!* (2007). This setting apart is not a case of elevated genre, a recent concept in criticism and reviewing akin to vulgar auteurism, where writers seek to lift disreputable films or those dismissed by consensus out of the mire and into the light. George Miller eventually made pictures in Hollywood, winning acclaim and awards. He has directed 10 films in 40 years, including two successful animated features about singing and dancing penguins (*Happy Feet* (2006) and *Happy Feet Two* (2011)). Add to this, the dark *Babe* (1995) sequel, *Babe: Pig in the City* (1998), *The Witches of Eastwick* (1987), *Lorenzo's Oil* (1992). In 1983, he contributed a short for the infamous *Twilight Zone: The Movie*, a big budget Steven Spielberg-backed extravaganza, which led to the deaths of actor Vic Morrow and two child actors, during the filming of John Landis' segment. Miller also directed or produced several acclaimed mini-series for Australian television. Nobody else in Ozploitation went on to have such a garlanded career, or became a maestro of action cinema. They remained firmly in low budget production, whether in Australia or abroad. It is tempting to place Peter Weir and Bruce Beresford alongside Miller, as all three got their start making genre pictures for local markets in the 1970s, but neither directed a giant success like *Mad Max*. Weir disappeared into American prestige pictures, and while Beresford scored big with *Driving Miss Daisy* (1989), his career generally defined by middle-of-the-road dross.

As a genre title made in Melbourne, as a guerrilla production made by newbies on a wing and a prayer, yes, it's Ozploitation. Not to disparage other low-budget movies of the era, but the reason *Mad Max* broke out as an international phenomenon was down to it being different from the rest. There is something, however, going on with this film. What other Ozploitation film made blockbuster money, became iconic and whose lead character in the sequels became Australia's answer to John Wayne, or Clint Eastwood's The Man with No Name? Ozploitation does, as an umbrella term, help give focus on a neglect strand of 1970s Australian genre filmmaking, and that can only be a good thing, even if the term is complicated in its relation to *Mad Max*.

The birth of the Australian New Wave was a seismic enough event to benefit *Mad Max*, though, unlike other projects, it was not the beneficiary of funding from the government's film bank initiatives. The Victoria Film Commission offered financing, but the filmmakers ended up sniffing out private dough from stock market traders, those looking for a tax-deductible investment, people with money burning a hole in their pockets and folk wealthy enough to take a punt. An intermediate named Noel Harman, a stockbroker by trade, helped Kennedy and Miller secure the money they needed, working out that thirty investors chipping in AU$10,000 each would see them over the line. If the film earned AU$1.5 million, everybody would be happy with the return on their investment. It's easy enough to imagine those who stumped up the money to make *Mad Max* got rich doing so. Neither Miller or Kennedy took any money upfront for writing-directing and producing duties.

Mad Max is indebted to a range of cinema influences and its storytelling form is classical. The western, 1950s teen rebel flicks and cop thrillers (Steven McQueen's 1968 flick, *Bullitt*, introduced the idea of a cool cop with a cooler car) flavour the soup. Miller the director is a little bit like the Main Force Patrol's Barry the Mechanic

(David Cameron), who builds the black-on-black V8, lifting 'a piece from here, a piece from there.' Yet its Australian identity is strong: the slang-strewn dialogue ('Very toey,' 'You'd better send a meat truck,' 'It's the duck's guts!') and the quintessentially Aussie anti-authoritarian streak running through the film, which allowed Miller and co-writer James McCausland to inject satiric jibes at the police into proceedings and a crucial nihilism, does not relate to American cinema at all. Two films, *The Cars That Ate Paris* and the biker movie *Stone* (1974), are forebearers and this was picked up on at the time of release. Colin Bennett, writing for The Australian four days after the film opened in Melbourne, where he reviewed William Friedkin's *The Brink's Job* (1978) and *Mad Max*, under the headline *Crime Pays for Idiots*, described the film's debt to the earlier films: 'It has a bizarre, striking quality visual style that combines the Hell's Angels elements of *Stone* with the doomsday mystique of *The Cars That Ate Paris*.'

Stone and *The Cars That Ate Paris* exhibit certain characteristics shared with *Mad Max*. All feature figures or groups acting outside the law and all three revel in anti-authoritarian attitudes. Although Sandy Harbutt's Stone lacks finesse and the kind of eye-catching compositions which make the work of Miller and Weir stand out, they are after all masters of the medium, announcing their tremendous skill with their first pictures, it nevertheless boasts a scuzzy charm and is a classic, and indeed pioneering, slice of Ozploitation.

Sandy Harbutt's *Stone*, released in June 1974, is the story of an outsider cop (played by Ken Shorter) going undercover with a gang of Sydney-based bikers (the Grave Diggers Motorcycle Club). Several of their crew have been murdered by assassins unknown and it's up to Stone (Shorter) to crack the case. Over the course of the film, a bond grows between the posh lawman and the crooked bikers. He undergoes an initiation ceremony, helps them fight against rivals and uncovers a conspiracy, but *Stone* upends this notion of two camps (the lawman and the crook) finding common cause with a cruel and savage sting in the tail (one which still shocks 45 years on). The final scene is the definition of brutal and Harbutt totally intended to leave a bad taste in the audience's mouth, just as Miller would comment on the spiritual and emotional emptiness felt by Max after exacting his revenge. The Main Force Patrol officer might have sated his appetite for revenge, but the victor feels less than victorious.

Among the cast of *Stone* are faces who'd crop up later in *Mad Max*, Hugh Keays-Byrne took a scenery-chewing supporting role as LSD-loving Toad, a performance which feels like a precursor to Toecutter. The scene in the biker bar, where he quietly harasses two gentlemen who've made the mistake of entering a place where they're not wanted, expertly upping the ante of discomfort while maintaining his cool, resonates in his captivating approach to Toecutter. Vince Gil (the Nightrider), Roger Ward (Fifi, Max's boss), Reg Evans (the Stationmaster) and David Bracks (Toecutter gang member Mudguts) also appeared in *Stone*. Most notably in its relation to *Mad Max*, Stone features a character named 'Bad Max'. Inspired by this, Miller made an alliterative alteration and came up with the title for his own film.

It is often claimed *Mad Max* was the first Australian picture to shoot in anamorphic widescreen. In fact, that was Peter Weir's Panavision-shot *The Cars That Ate Paris*. In a plot which would directly inspire British comedy television series *The League of Gentlemen*, Weir's blackly comic drama sees a gormless and timid young man, named Arthur Waldo (Terry Camilleri), stranded in the countryside and manipulated into staying by locals who are not what they seem. It is revealed the townsfolk are deliberately causing car crashes and then selling salvaged and scavenged parts. And business is booming! Among the cast is Bruce Spence, who would later star in *Mad Max 2* as the Gyro Captain and, somewhat confusingly, as Jedediah the Pilot in *Mad Max Beyond Thunderdome*.

As Miller recognised when it came time to shoot *Mad Max*, the sheer size of Australian landscapes screams for widescreen cinematography. *The Cars That Ate Paris* had a photographic potency new to Australian cinema. The landscapes, the hills, the trees, the quiet country lanes achieve a haunting quality close to the shores of the horror movie and in general rings with a dreamy gothic atmosphere. *Mad Max* and *The Cars That Ate Paris* also share a post-colonial reflection on the inglorious triumph of European, western lifestyles and technology over an ancient land with one of the longest continued civilizations known to history (notwithstanding the almost complete absence of First Australians in the *Mad Max* series). It is a variation on the theme of paradise lost or paradise squandered. While the focus is on human drama, the landscapes do not merely serve as a colourful backdrop, but underline the pessimistic subtexts of each film as nightmare visions of settler society and cultural degradation.

Max's Politics

Fifi: 'They say people don't believe in heroes anymore. Well, damn them! You and me, Max, we're gonna give 'em back their heroes.'

Max: 'Do you really expect me to go for that crap?'

Before we delve into Phillip Adams' infamous magazine attack against *Mad Max* (titled 'The dangerous pornography of death'), which appeared in The Bulletin (May 1979), it's worth noting that the cultural reaction to *Mad Max* made politicians take notice and there were calls in the Australian Parliament for the film to be banned. Today, we might be mad for Max and Australia may see the character and mythology as something to celebrate, but back in 1979 the reaction wasn't so open-armed and all-embracing. Of course, negative reviews or moral panic campaigns failed to stop *Mad Max* from becoming a box-office juggernaut, but people who hated it registered their disgust vehemently. To them, *Mad Max* wasn't any old genre garbage to be dismissed outright and consigned to the bin, it was deemed politically suspect and deserved a merciless interrogation. Max all too readily descends to the level of the villains in order to exact his calculated and methodical revenge plan against a group of bikers. The young lawman becomes an avenging husband and father. His thirst will not be sated until Toecutter and his gang are all dead. This bloodthirsty creed isn't how police officers are supposed to behave in the movies. Max uses his badge, police-issue car, uniform and gun when he takes out the proverbial trash. It's little wonder liberals saw Miller's character as fascistic and reactionary, but Miller was aware what he was taking on in making his protagonist a hellbent copper.

Max's campaign of killing ends with a wicked coup de grace, one designed to maximise a person's sense of helplessness and terror. Handcuffing Johnny the Boy to a car wreck and setting up an explosion, Max throws him a hacksaw and tells the drug-addled psycho he can cut through human bone in 5 minutes or through steel in 10 minutes (Doctor George would know). The guy is toast either way, and we might venture Max is getting off on the distress he is causing the sole-surviving Toecutter goon. He's methodical, to the point of robotic, a man going through the motions of vengeance. Leaving Johnny to fry in the imminent explosion is not how a screen hero should act, right? It invites us to relish in the lad's anguish. Or does it? Being appalled by Max's actions is an equally valid response. But this can get confused with a director endorsing his creation's behaviour. This was a charge levelled at Don Siegel, when he directed *Dirty Harry* (1971). The scene with Max and Johnny the Boy is barbarous and goes beyond a man seeking righteous justice. Contradictions and thematic messiness further abound as Miller satirises the white hat and black hat American western archetypes, turning the white hat (Max) into the black hat (Mad Max). It's very different in the sequels, where Max's actions are rendered as sentimental tragedy. In the original film, Max goes berserk and snuffs out the villains with his own brand of justice.

The 1970s was awash with maverick cop and vigilante figures on television and movie screens. *Dirty Harry* is king of maverick law enforcement, but Max could be his young deputy, and what a spin-off that pairing could have been (tagline: Bad Cop meets Mad Cop). Don Siegel's controversial thriller introduced a policeman to the movies whose lone wolf creed and penchant for Third-Degree policing led to charges of crypto fascism. The police badge imbuing the protagonist with an immense feeling of power and by-any-means-necessary policing. How could liberal Hollywood make such a vile picture, critics asked? Director Siegel argued they were missing the point. He neither condoned nor celebrated Harry's style of justice. Harry was a representation of our darker impulses and Old Testament leanings.

In Miller's film, car culture replaces America's gun culture. It's a crucial distinction, as Max's V8 Interceptor is the totem of masculinity; Dirty Harry Callaghan's is the obviously phallic Smith & Wesson Model 29.44 Magnum (the 1973 sequel to *Dirty Harry* was even called *Magnum Force*). Callaghan likes to dick swing about how powerful his weapon is: 'I know what you're thinking "Did he fire 6 shots or only 5?" Well, to tell the truth, in all this excitement, I've kinda lost track myself. But this being a .44 Magnum, the most powerful handgun in the world, and would blow your head clean off, you've got to ask yourself one question: "Do you feel lucky?" Well, do ya, punk?'

Harry became the poster cop for right-wing blowhards. He wasn't a bad apple in the San Francisco Police Department, it was the bureaucrats, the pencil-pushers, the wimps who were all wrong. They hadn't a clue what it's like out there, in the urban jungle, where the scum rises and thrives, preying on the innocent. In this line of thinking, toilet cleaners like Harry Callaghan or, indeed, Max Rockatansky, need to give the world a good flush. *Mad Max* doesn't really trade in this kind of reactionary nonsense, more flirts with it for satirical purpose, though one of the earliest advertising campaigns for its release in Melbourne picture-houses announced as a tagline:

'When the gangs take over the highway ...

... Remember he's on your side.'

Max was sold as a true hero, but he's anything but. The tough cop in leather was window-dressing for Miller's comic-book concept in what is a film of post-modernist-style bricolage. It's understandable enough to see why *Mad Max*'s aping of perceived right-wing rhetoric alarmed some, but Miller wasn't remotely interested in expressing any serious political point. If anything, he was taking the piss. This is very apparent in a series of sight gags dotted throughout the film. The framed photo of Queen Elizabeth II in the office at the Halls of Justice, the pig windchime on the porch at Max's beachfront home, cops appearing buffoonish (Roop and Charlie in the opening chase) and the blink-and-you'll-miss-it shot of Sprog playing with Max's gun unsupervised (whether it's loaded or not is a question left unanswered). Max is the guy with the highest body count and kill streak, too. Freeing us from complicated reactions to murder, morality and empathy is a nihilistic method and viewpoint seen frequently in action movies and television. It isn't healthy and Miller is aware of it – he built his film on a man losing his humanity. Dirty Harry would shoot a perp dead, then go and eat a hotdog like it was all nothing but a thing. Max is struggling to hold on and, once he lets go, finds himself driven to savage acts and turning his back on the world.

Miller's remit was never the same as Don Siegel's. The latter deliberately toyed with button-pushing reactions to the counter-culture revolution, where underneath San Fran's Summer of Love image was a world of vice and things happening that were far from groovy. The Zodiac Killer was loose at the time of the film's release, taunting the press and the police with bizarre letters. A few years earlier, Charlie Manson had recruited impressionable middle-class kids for his apocalypse cult, from hippie

The pig windchime on Max's porch highlights the film's satiric streak and classic Aussie attitude to mocking authority.

epicentre Haight and Ashbury. But *Mad Max* had no such socio-political ambition or comment to make on Australian crime statistics or the law. Miller and Kennedy were not imparting a worldview that was deliberately reactionary or right-wing, nor were they contending that Victoria Police and wider Australia policing could do with a few more like Max out on the roads. They exploited, maybe cynically, the popular image of the lone cop operating in a savage world.

Max the Man

Does Max Rockatansky represent a new breed of hero? As suggested – no, not really. His heroic attributes only emerged in the sequels. But what kind of man is Max? Through the screenplay and Mel Gibson's performance, we can glean certain psychological details about the bloke behind the badge and his masculine (indeed, human) reaction to having things taken away from him. We know he is self-aware enough to tell Fifi his concerns about going over the edge and becoming a hoon. The film's social anxiety dovetails well into the personal anxieties experienced by Max. He is a guy barely out of his teens, working a dangerous job, married, and father to a little boy. Max isn't burning the candles at both ends, but is a cop attuned to the troubles of the world around him who fears they will eventually impact him (of course he isn't aware how massively this will come to pass). He sees his job first and foremost as protecting Jess and Sprog, taking them away after Goose's death, tossing in the MFP badge and believing he can outrun his troubles. There is something distinctly sentimental and traditional in the man's attitudes.

To provide Max with character depth beyond his role as MFP's finest and family man, Miller inserted a scene with Jess, after they've fled Melbourne and its environs in the wake of Goose's death. In this scene, Max discusses his father and how he looked up to him. It's a tender moment in a series not exactly known for such focus. Slam, bam action, yes, but soulful reflection? Not really. Lying in the grass on a picnic blanket, Jess in his arms, Max relates how men often hide their feelings and how things left unspoken produce regret and sadness. This ghostly image we get of Max's father (a man without a face walking in long strides in shiny brown shoes) is unique. Max, of course, becomes haunted by the deaths of those he loved, but this memory of his old man is different. In other words, Max does not want to be a typical bloke and wishes to articulate his emotions in a masculine culture which frowns upon men displaying any. The memory of his father leads into Max telling Jess how much he loves her. The scene occurs right before events lead up to her death, making their intimacy more devastating; at least, that is the intended dramatic effect. The *Mad Max* series isn't noted for psychological realism or depth of character beyond archetypal portraits, but, again, the original movie sticks out because it does things the others do not do, because it's not yet set in a post-apocalyptic hell-world. Max tells Jess:

'When I was a kid, me and my father used to go for long walks. I remember staring down at his shoes. They were special shoes – brown – and he always kept them shiny. He was tall, and he used to take long strides, and there I'd be right alongside him … just trying to keep up with him. I don't think he ever knew how proud I felt of him or how good it felt just to be there alongside him. Even now, when I think back on it, I still feel … The thing is, Jess … I couldn't tell him about it then, but I can tell you about it now. I don't want to wait years to tell you how I'm feeling about you right now.'

Max being an emotionless, reluctant hero works in the sequels, but it wouldn't work at all in the original film. Max lashing out and avenging the dead aren't heroic actions, they are ultimately selfish, derived from Old Testament morality, especially 'An eye for an eye'. But the origin of Max's pain does open the door to his heroism.

We know Miller did not have any ideas for sequels at the time of the film's inception or filming. But retroactively, *Mad Max* served as an origins story. Without the anchor of family and friendship, a man is nothing. Following Max's journey in the film from young father and husband to killer, the adventures he faces in the sequels offer shots at redemption and respite from the emotionless void.

Critical Reception

Critical big guns such as the late Time critic, Richard Corliss, saw *Mad Max* at the Cannes Film Festival and championed the work, recognising specifically Miller's directorial flair and skills in montage:

> The hardware is the star here: the souped-up Chevies and demon motorcycles, captured by Miller's supple, fender-level camera--one machine in sync with another. With his instinct and craft, Miller has provided more autosuggestive violence on a $1 million budget than *The Blues Brothers* did with half the Chicago police force and $30 million. (1980: 92)

But as detailed in the introduction, not all critics appreciated the film (to put it mildly). Mary McDonald, of the Courier-Mail newspaper, listed the film's achievements – 10 nominations at the Australian film awards, extraordinary levels of sales to overseas markets, its filmmaking precision – but said that all those things amounted to nothing. In McDonald's eyes, the film had been all 'style with no soul'. That's code for: They wanted to make money, lots of money, the dirty capitalists! It isn't art.

Writing for The Telegraph in September 1979, Stuart Scott's dismissal of the movie is hilarious. The review begins with an existentialist jibe and rolls out the punches. 'I wasted one night of my life this week... I went to see *Mad Max*. It is 1 ½ hours of nonsense. And poorly made, poorly written and poorly acted nonsense at that. I can't think of any movie to beat it for sheer silliness.' After a brief rundown of the film's plot, which he of course thinks stupid, the one positive Scott admitted was 'it's not boring'. He goes on to say: 'The characters make no visible attempt to act, the story wanders along in vague fashion; much of the dialogue is lost to the musical soundtrack which is a notch or two too loud.' To top it all off, Scott is positively flummoxed by the film's growing popularity. He of course put it down to sheer curiosity value. '*Mad Max* is, incredibly, a great success,' Scott complained,

> It's one of two Australian movies doing well down south (the other is *My Brilliant Career*, yet to reach us), and the night I went along the George was packed. But it's the sort of film that will attract crowds just want to see what it's about, determined to find out for themselves. Don't say you weren't warned.

Written a few months earlier, Brian White's review in *The Mirror* was apoplectic, making Scott's look the voice of reason. Rarely today would a genre film cause so much blind moral panic and snobbery. As with other reviewers, *Mad Max* was fair game since it openly aped and exploited American cinema, therefore culturally suspect and inherently inferior to Hollywood product. As well as referring to audience enjoyment as 'bestial', White described a moment everybody cheered as akin to Coliseum patrons watching a lion 'having a good chew on a Christian' and his overall summary is bizarrely coloured by the previous film he saw that day: Terrence Malick's 1978 opus, *Days of Heaven*. In White's summary, George Miller's movie is utter trash, Malick's is high art.

Mad Max faces the censors and media

The debate on the issue of screen violence and bad behaviour influencing unhinged minds had previously been prominent back in the mid-1950s, with the rise of the Hollywood youth picture and a previously invisible demographic, the teenager, finding a voice. Before that, it was political movies which censor boards thought might agitate the working classes and turn them into Marxist-Leninist revolutionaries. *Mad Max*, with its cinematic sound and fury, as well as its filmmaking clout, was bound to appeal to young audiences wanting the latest cinematic thrill. But would it then transform them into hoons?

The Australian Crime Prevention Council's deputy president, Andrew Johnson, also a federal member of parliament for Brisbane, drew direct parallels with 1950s classics and Stanley Kubrick's controversial *A Clockwork Orange* (1972). 'Even though it was made in Australia, it should be banned in Australia,' Johnson told the Courier Mail (21 May 1979). After mentioning Miller's film made Phillip Adams 'physically ill with revulsion', Johnson stated: 'In the fifties we had *The Blackboard Jungle* and *Rebel Without a Cause* and, in the early seventies, *A Clockwork Orange*.' Johnson then went on to say he was going to ask the Queensland film censor to take a gander at the film and hopefully remove it from theatres.

History repeatedly shows that there is nothing a politician likes more than to get on a bandwagon and save the nation from sicko works of art, which they rarely understand or attempt to contextualise. The West Australian further reported Johnson's objections to the film (22 May 1979): 'This film contained scenes of pack rape, the burning of traffic policemen and the running down of children, which only a small number of Australians could consider worthwhile entertainment.' Johnson's biggest fear was that the movie would achieve a cult following.

In New Zealand, the government film censorship office slapped a ban on *Mad Max*, which remained in place until 1983, despite the sequel *Mad Max 2* being released there uncut in 1981 (both received R18 certificates). In 1980, distributor Twentieth Century Fox appealed the original decision, but it was upheld by New Zealand's Films Censorship Board of Review. George Miller flew over to make an appearance before the board and state his case, but no dice. Board chairperson, Judge Tony Beatson, told The Australian the ban would remain 'because of the nature and degree of violence portrayed... it's likely to be injurious to the public'.

The reason often cited for the ban is a real-life case said to mimic the death of Goose. A report in the Canberra Times (5 July 1980) brought up the similarity between Jim Goose's murder and an event in August 1979, where a gang of Maori bikers went on the rampage over a territorial dispute with rival outfits. During a riot fuelled by alcohol and a stockpile of resentments, the bikers attempted to set fire to a New Zealand copper. But as with most urban myths which become fact in the telling, there is no direct evidence that this supposed convergence of life imitating art played any significant part in the judge's subsequent decision-making process. It draws an imaginary link between the gang having watched the film and being directly inspired by it. What the censors found more concerning was the overall level of violence found in Miller's movie. Judge Beatson contended that to have *Mad Max* on general release would provoke mayhem amongst certain sections of society. 'The irresponsible attitude of bikie gangs in New Zealand at the moment meant the film could have a harmful effect on certain elements of the public.'

Mad Max is a violent film. Even its sound effects – the growling engines, the metal on metal crunch – were designed to unnerve and provide intensity. There are flashes of gore, but blood and guts are not splattered across the screen any more than in Tobe Hooper's seminal horror classic, *The Texas Chain Saw Massacre* (1974). The reaction to both films was so visceral, audiences and critics alike believed they'd seen much more on-screen than they in fact did. The secret is in the montage and the subliminal-like effect it produced. In his review for The Sun (5 July 1979), headlined '*Mad Max* … it's a stunner!' John Hanrahan made a perceptive point, regarding the editing. 'It is not a blatantly violent film, indeed, much of the violence is implied rather than spread across the screen.' David Stratton was another critic at the time who wrote in his Variety mag review 'plenty of horror is implied.'

For The Guardian (UK), Derek Malcolm made a similar observation, in what is a rave review:

> The most astonishing Australian debut since that country's new wave hit us several years ago. Astonishing because it is totally unlike anything else from Australia, being a brilliantly-orchestrated road-cum-horror movie with the sorts of stunts Hollywood (Roger Corman at any rate) would envy … The film has very little direct violence in it, though a great deal is suggested. What it is, above all, is a supremely cinematic montage, an animated Marvel comic, which is exploitative, but clearly the work of a natural film-maker.

Elsewhere around the world, even in such a famously liberal country as France, *Mad Max* was slapped with the X certificate and removed from circulation by Warner Bros., unhappy with the scale of taxes on foreign titles but also conscious of the limit on the number of X-rated movies that theatres would play in France at that time. Two years later, it was re-cut (losing seven minutes and twenty-three seconds) and sent out to 120 French picture banned X rating now reclassified. The film's fate and journey to the screen in France is a strange one. The censors were worried about 'excessive violence' and Le Matin newspaper erroneously reported two stuntmen had died.

Sweden, like New Zealand, slapped a ban on it outright. The Scandinavian country was among the first places in the world to set up a censorship office and it remained in place until 2011, when a law was passed scrapping it altogether. The Statens biografbyrå did eventually lift the ban on *Mad Max* in 2005.

Max and the BBFC

In Britain, the BBFC (British Board of Film Censors, later British Board of Film Classification) reports have been released online related to certification on two separate occasions (for the initial theatrical run and the 1992 VHS release), enabling us to look at what the organisation found problematic and how time and cultural attitudes reflected subsequent changes. Examiners found the movie to be 'tough' but 'discreet' in relation to the on-screen violence, noting most of the violence was carried out on objects (cars) rather than people. The examiner's note is undated, but the film was given a certificate on 14 August 1979. The report acknowledged the film's aesthetic virtuosity and added the film wowed critics at the 1979 Cannes Film Festival. The examiner, however, finds potential problems with the violence:

> The impression of extreme violence is achieved largely through spectacular effects and brilliant stunt work [but] the gang's terrorising of the young couple whose car they have forced off the road seemed excessive, and a dangerous model of violent behaviour to offer to the sort of audience who might find themselves attracted to this sort of entertainment.

Mad Max was passed with the 'X' certificate after 49 seconds of cuts made to said offending scene. The specific instruction was to 'reduce to absolute minimum smashing up of car and terrorising of young couple who are trapped in it. Delete all destructive violence which occurs after gang break in the window, resuming on the bird hovering overhead.'

Miller's film had been released on videotape prior to the passing of the 1984 Video Recordings Act and was submitted again by Warner Brothers Home Video Limited, as per requirements by law, receiving the new '18' certificate (dated 10 April 1986) with the 49 seconds of cuts still in place. In 1992, the film came up again for certification, this time passed fully uncut. The BBFC scoring card offers a fascinating insight into censorship and how times change. What was problematic or unacceptable back in 1979 or 1986 appeared to have dissipated by 1992, as a sign of changing sensibilities and sensitivities. Yet the theme of 'terrorisation' still bothered the BBFC enough.

The score card used by the BBFC examiner is set out in columns. Down the side, on the far left, is a set of categorisations which correspond to the certificate levels 'Uc', 'U', 'PG', '15', '18' and the category for pornography, 'R18', listed along the top. Categories are listed as 'Theme', 'Treatment', 'Visuals: Nudity, Sex, Violence, Sexual Violence, Horror'. Also forming the score card are topics such as 'Language, Drugs, Imitable Techniques, Legality: Obscenity, Children, Animals', 'Blasphemy' and 'Film as a whole'. The suggested certification is given as '18', though overall, it achieved three Xs in the '15' category (for 'Theme, Sex and Language') and only two in the '18' ('Treatment and Violence').

Under the comments section, the examiner first noted that the reintroduction of the original Australian dialogue much improved the quality of the film: 'Greatly improved with the original voices. It will be even more improved by laying off cutting this, as there are no strong arguments against what is in this tape in toto,' the examiner begins.

Studying the once-offending scene, the BBFC goes over it again, this time declaring there's nothing much to get too het up about. 'Both the man and woman have probably been raped, though only the man shows physical evidence of this', adding that the power of the scene comes from point of view shots from inside the couple's car as the windows are smashed. 'None of this strays into territory of sexual titillation, since it is only by inference and not explicitly that the viewer would "know" that rapes occurred. DEATH WISH [examiner's capitalisation] this is most definitely not.'

The examiner concluded the memo/report by recommending the film be passed with the '18' certificate and should be uncut.

Phillip Adams and 'the dangerous pornography of death'

It's the article above all others written at the time of the film's release, which many hardcore fans and scholars of the movie will have heard about or read. Phillip Adams was so outraged by *Mad Max*, his first port of call, after attending a press preview screening, was to contact the Australian Film Commission, asking if the government had put any money into the blasted thing. If they had indeed ploughed cold hard cash into George Miller's action opus, he believed heads would roll. To say he was incensed is an understatement, Phillip Adams was fuming like a Looney Tunes cartoon with flames coming out of his ears. But there was a personal dimension to the pasting he doled out, a sort of revenge against Miller, for a perceived slight a few years earlier.

Mad Max, he wrote in The Bulletin (1 May 1979), had the moral uplift of Hitler's *Mein Kampf* and he goes on to write how the film will be a favourite with 'rapists, sadists, child-murderers, Mansons and Calleys'. Adams didn't leave it at that. He added, mockingly, anything he said against the film would be taken by Al Finney, publicist for distributor Village Roadshow, and cynically quoted on film posters, to drum up more business. What galled him so? While Adams had a bee in his bonnet (and does to this day) about screen violence and its effects on society, entirely valid as an intellectual standpoint, he also appeared to enjoy the pugilistic relationship he had with the movie and George Miller. Since 1979, he hasn't let go or toned down his whinging against either Miller or the *Mad Max* series. Like others, he admired Miller's craftsmanship, but remained somewhat dismayed by what he crafted.

Headlined 'The dangerous pornography of death', The Bulletin piece was intended not just as a rebuke, but the presentation of a mini thesis on the inherent vice of action cinema. Like those who rallied against Video Nasties in 1980s Britain, Adams saw violence on the screen as a trigger for impressionable or corruptible minds (though he never questioned his own exposure, as if he and others are made of sterner stuff). He brings up Kubrick's *A Clockwork Orange* as an example of how a movie influenced real-life cases of violent behaviour, praising Kubrick for having the sense to not let his own kids see it (the ex-pat director removed his satirical drama from circulation in the UK). He also collared Nicholas Ray's *Rebel Without a Cause* (1955) for introducing the game of 'chicken' onto Aussie roads. He lamented, too, that *The Blackboard Jungle* (1951) singlehandedly shipped over teenage delinquency to the country as a sort of cultural take on Brits shipping their undesirables to Australia, back in the days when it was a penal colony.

When *Mad Max: Fury Road* was released in May 2015, to widespread critical acclaim, Adams wrote a piece for The Australian, telling readers early on how he'd walked out after 20 minutes because he couldn't take the film's 'genial genocide', as he referred to it. He missed out on all the good stuff! But how on earth could he write about a film where he openly admits to storming out the exit after the opening act? Adams still positioned himself as an imperious teller of truths:

> I thought *Mad Max* some sort of masterpiece, far and away the best directed film of our new wave. Which made me loathe it all the more. Working on a tiny budget, long before the era of digital delusions, George showed himself a genius for what the droogs in Kubrick's *A Clockwork Orange* would describe as a 'bit of ultraviolence'. Never had I seen executions so beautifully executed, savagery so exquisitely choreographed. And what happened when my protests appeared in print? George and Byron proudly quoted them in their ads.

Even Adams admits it was superior to anything else produced in the era, New Wave or Ozploitation, furthering the argument, it stands alone in 1970s Aussie cinema.

Adams looks like he's showcasing, in print, an overbearing paternalistic worry about an errant son (Miller), thus positioning himself the Father of the New Wave? Adams whined on: 'Whilst Kubrick suffered some agonies of doubt about the social impact of *A Clockwork Orange* (too many real-life thugs mimicking his) and withdrew it from UK screens, George remains impervious to wowsers like me and keeps upping the ante. The cruelty in the original's plot, which put the most vulnerable characters in harm's way, is replaced by sheer momentum, with only a vestigial hint of morality. It's a non-stop joust of juggernauts and sub-human flotsam wherein the newly minted Max mutters menacingly while his female counterpart, a Ms Furiosa, mows 'em down in the millions. And everyone loves it.'

Phillip Adams did his bit to get the Aussie film industry up and running again in the late 1960s and into the 1970s. It was his government report in the late 1960s, which heralded a sea change in the industry. But his envisioning of a respectable Australian cinema certainly did not include genre movies like *Mad Max*, no matter how much he professed to admire Miller's filmmaking craft. For the truth of the matter is Adams took umbrage with Miller and Kennedy before he'd seen it. Adams thought the pair were taking the piss out of him with their acclaimed short film, *Violence in the Cinema, Part I*. He admitted this in The Australian article's introduction.

> Their first film, 20 minutes of mounting mayhem called *Violence in the Cinema Part 1*, won oodles of festival awards. It was a cultural manifesto, a declaration of war. It depicted a rather boring man pontificating on media violence at a conference. As he speaks, he is stabbed, sliced, diced and finally eviscerated. Until all that's left is a bloodied mouth that keeps droning on. Arthur Dignam played the part. He was playing me. (Adams, 2015)

According to the article, he was approached by potential Mad Max investors, who sought to consult him about signing up to the project. Adams warned them off, cautioning that participating in the production would be disastrous. Adams gave his reasoning as thus: the stunts were beyond the technical capability of stuntmen working Down Under, he doubted Miller could pull off what he envisioned in his head and – the most revealing of all – the idea for an Aussie biker movie made him 'morally queasy'. He cited the fact drive-ins had been full of gratuitously violent flickers and the Miller-Kennedy project was a cynical bid to exploit and cash in on a fad. Adams referred directly to the works of Roger Corman, Don Siegel and Sam Peckinpah as the worst offenders of the lot. Adams also stated, incorrectly, that the film's stunts were performed by an authentic biker gang and not a professional stunt crew, which included Grant Page, a technician who'd go on to become an industry legend. Adams credited controversial artist Ivan Durrant with designing amputated limbs and gory special effects (again, not true).

In his attempt to give *Mad Max* a good kicking, Adams produced an article one-part revenge piece and a poor attempt at social studies, opportunistically using Miller's hit film as a target and punchbag. Adams isn't 'thinking of the children'; he suggested Miller should have had his characters (thus inferring people he refers to as 'delinquents') play Russian Roulette, as in Michael Cimino's *The Deer Hunter* (1979). 'Then he'd be lowering the delinquent population without increasing the road toll.' The social snobbery is eye-popping.

Adams seems mystified by the fact screen violence is popular and that it can be thrilling, enjoyable and cathartic, rather than inherently damaging to a person's mind or wider society. Poppy Z. Brite noted in her essay 'The Poetry of Violence', that the inference for audiences who enjoy a bit of violence on the big screen is they are suspect people, subhuman at worst and deviant at best. *Mad Max* is not necessarily about the poetry of violence, but there is poetry in its staging of action and use of montage. Brite explained the appeal of screen violence:

> The poetry of violence is loathed by many and denied by even more. Violence cannot encompass beauty, claim these squeamish souls; by its very nature violence is crude, base, evil, and nothing but. Those of us who savour it, even on paper or film, are probably evil too: we've surrendered our humanity for a peek at someone's innards. (Brite, 1996: 63-64)

CHAPTER THREE: THE WHITE LINE NIGHTMARE

George Miller's unique take on the car chase

The *Mad Max* franchise is known for its epic car chases, and we might say, in general, Australian filmmakers are cinema's leading experts of car crashes. Car chases, crashes and staging furious action is where Miller's creative genius kick in. In a current filmmaking trend tending towards gravity-defying imagery and extensive use of green-screen, Miller's *Mad Max* movies are far from the weightless spectacle dominating our screens, nor are they reliant on suspension of disbelief. The director told Los Angeles Daily News reporter, Rob Lowman, in a May 2015 discussion of *Mad Max: Fury Road*: 'It doesn't defy the laws of physics.' This rule, call it a philosophy, was implemented from the first movie and it's been revised on a grander and grander scale with the subsequent sequels, though never losing the grounded sense of perspective. *Mad Max* movies are set in a blighted future hellscape, but the action is realistic. None of the cars, trucks or bikes perform stunts or manoeuvres which stretch credulity or ask for the suspense of disbelief. In Miller's films, vehicles do not perform acts of which they are physically incapable as machines.

Miller orchestrates chaos like no other director. What's intriguing, what sets him apart from other directors, is not just his bravura use of practical effects and mounting dangerous-looking stunts for real, but how dangerous they can be in the world of the movie. In other words, unexpected elements are thrown in to liven up proceedings and keep the audience hooked into the virtuosic storytelling. Cause and effect crop up all the time; often having devastating impacts on a character, sets of characters and their vehicles. These scenes of metal crunching carmageddon look uncontrolled and uncontrollable. Miller and his crew make things look like bedlam, but it's all finely tuned, deliberate and orchestrated to appear out of control. What's particularly mind-blowing regarding the first film is that the director did not use storyboards. Compare it to *Mad Max: Fury Road*, which discarded the traditional script in favour of storyboards, and *Mad Max*'s production without storyboarding the action sequences looks positively bonkers; every image, every shot was in Miller's head. While *Mad Max*'s action quota is positively quaint, when compared to the rest of the series, the director's debut demonstrates the beginnings of an action schema that has had a huge influence on car chases ever since.

As mentioned, Miller likes to throw in curveballs during chase sequences. We see it in *Mad Max*'s opening chase with the caravan stuck in the middle of the road and the toddler wandering away from his mother. In the sequels, Miller took things to even giddier heights. In *Mad Max 2*, during a high-speed pursuit (Max is driving a rig back to the oil compound, through a sea of petrolhead goons, swarming like wasps), a mechanic is accidentally crushed beneath a car he's been working on. The deadly outcome occurs entirely by chance, when Max swipes a pursuing marauder, knocking it off course and banging into the vehicle the mechanic is tinkering with. Another good example is The Gyro Captain dropping a snake onto a Lord Humungus gang member manning a multi-arrowed shooting device. The shock of a snake landing on him causes the gunner to shoot his driver, the vehicle then careens into a stacked formation of burned-out cars. *Mad Max* car chases are wild with details not found in other types of action cinema. Miller always was, to use a cliché, thinking outside the box. His chases are ruled by Hitchcockian suspense, playful red herrings and ironic visual gags. The contagious nihilism of this free-for-all mayhem is what gives *Mad Max* films their potent juice. There is no such thing as collateral damage, everybody and every precious resource is expendable. Only in a world gone mad would the pursuit of an object or goal, pointless or not, be so single-mindedly engaged.

Action cinema as visual rock 'n' roll

In 12 gloriously high-octane minutes, George Miller would establish the founding tenets of his visual rock 'n' roll theory. In his 1997 BFI documentary, *40,000 Years of Dreaming*, he described his vision: 'I saw movies purely as visual music. *Mad Max* was like a piece of visual rock 'n' roll.' This aesthetic approach is something he would return to with every subsequent *Mad Max* picture until it resembled less a good old blast of three-chord rock 'n' roll and more a full-blown rock opera. 'I'm naturally a montage filmmaker,' Miller once explained, 'in the sense of the cumulative syntax of the individual shots within the composition of the lenses. It's why I love action movies. I see them as pure cinema' (Martin, 2003: 9).

The director told critic David Chute, in a 1982 Film Comment interview, how he believed Westerns had not died out, but had transformed into the 1970s cop thriller, the old west gunfight now a car chase. He discussed his view of editing and the diktats he followed.

> The process of sucking an audience into the screen must work on absolutely every level; on a mythological level and a sociological level – depending on the time and the history of that particular culture. It has to work on a psychological level and even a physiological level: how long can people sit without moving, how quickly can they absorb visual and sound information.

In the same interview, he went onto describe how he was inspired by silent movies. 'My rule in editing action is that you should cut it like a silent movie, so that if you watch it without sound you'll miss very little.' This is true, as an experiment, watch any of the *Mad Max* films with the sound off, and you'll be able to follow the storytelling easily enough.

Miller and his small editorial team spent a long time perfecting the overall rhythms and timings of shots. There are shots in the film which last barely a frame, while most average a couple of seconds during scenes and sequences of vehicles in motion. Miller's approach to staging action scenes, use of montage and sound design is constructed to produce an overwhelming sensory thrill. Compared to a lot of modern-day Hollywood cutting, which is downright ugly, we do not suffer information overload or get lost in terms of spatial continuity. Miller's prowess as a director with a fine eye for what cuts together was praised in an online filmed interview with Mel Gibson (Collider, October 2016). While promoting his latest directorial effort, *Hacksaw Ridge* (2016), the actor-turned-director referred to Miller as a scientist and the 'Einstein of Edit'. According to Gibson, Miller was a genius for his ability 'to get the pieces necessary to make a truly compelling action, in-your-face action sequence. He was always like that. I remember doing stuff with him and I didn't even understand what he was doing.'

Miller's use of montage merges Classical Hollywood editing with bits borrowed from Soviet-style montage. It owes a debt to DW Griffith's use of parallelism, but also the experimental ideas and methods of such pioneering film directors as Sergei

Eisenstein and Vsevolod Pudovkin. DW Griffith became famous for his pioneering use of parallelism, with films such as *The Birth of a Nation* (1915) and *Intolerance* (1916). Griffith didn't invent narrative and editing techniques, but he used them at a time when American cinema practitioners wished to drag the medium into the light of art. These innovations helped audiences become more sophisticated and alert to complex narratives. Cross-cutting produced bafflement in early cinema, but it provided a dynamism unique to the movies. Although constantly shifting between different actions and locations, continuity and coherence is provided and maintained by the logic of the scenario and by the construction of motive. 'Each parallel shot and sequence is based on a clear counter motive,' as Sam Rohdie described Griffith's concept of parallelism (Rohdie, 2006: 50).

The director saw the commercial American cinema as his guiding beacon to artistic success, but he no doubt would heartily agree with Pudovkin's position, that montage was the highest form of editing and the 'foundation of film art'. Miller would be on board, too, with Lev Kuleshov, the founding father of montage, who theorised in 1917: 'The essence of cinema lies in the film's composition i.e. in the exchange between photographed pieces for the organisation of impressions. What is most significant is not what is filmed in a specific shot, but how one shot replaces another on the screen, how they are structured in time sequence' (1980: 15).

Miller is very much a director of vivid effect through editing. It should be noted the words 'shooting' and 'cutting' are terms associated with violence yet often used to describe filmmaking procedures. These two words are subverted by cinema for pleasurable ends. Shooting and cutting are acts of destruction refigured as acts of creation. With George Miller, a trained medical physician, these words sound even more surgical and probing. Doctor Miller, the 'Ayatolla of the Moviola', 'the surgeon of the grotesque', as Film Comment's David Chute referred to the director in his 1982 review of *The Road Warrior*.

The marriage between east and west editing principles is made apparent in *Mad Max*'s opening chase, where a series of parallel happenings coincide with the introduction of the hero (teased in disembodied shots or wide shots). What's so arresting about the *Mad Max* car chase is that it appears at the start, when usually it's a centrepiece sequence or used in a finale. Miller wanted to make a statement and catch the viewer unaware. *Mad Max*'s opener grabs the attention of the audience immediately, throwing them in at the deep end, setting a standard and level of energy for the rest of the film to follow.

The setup at the start of the movie:

A maniac known as the Nightrider has escaped from police custody. The Nightrider is a member of Toecutter's gang (the letters T & C are inked on his face). He is fleeing the Main Force Patrol to reunite with his mates. Having stolen a Pursuit Special (a Holden HQ Monaro, 1972 model), the criminal is engaged in a chase with The March Hare (an MFP unit). The March Hare radio another team, letting them know the Nightrider is on their turf. Picking up the message is Charlie and Roop, whose vehicle is codenamed Big Bopper, and Max Rockatansky, who works alone.

The film establishes several points of action: The Nightrider attempting to flee the cops, Max's preparation for a deadly encounter and subsequent road duel, March Hare's pursuit, Big Bopper's pursuit, Goose's introduction and involvement in the chase, a baby wandering into the road, his mother and boyfriend caught up in a domestic argument, and a caravan driven by a holidaying couple getting stuck in the middle of the road.

Where Miller gets more experimental and where we find echoes of Soviet era montage is in the disembodied shots of Max, who is introduced as if being assembled and constructed before our eyes, like some sort of man-machine or a Frankenstein monster as maverick cop. Through the sequence of shots, if extrapolated from the rest of the opening chase, the use of extreme close-ups, wide shots, disembodied shots, medium shots, all craft an energy of emerging power and authority. We know Max will triumph where Big Bopper and March Hare have failed. It's all in the way he is presented. The close-ups of Max's sunglasses reflecting the land, speak of an authority, telling us the game is already up for the Nightrider before he and Max have met. Miller also follows an Eisenstein-style theory in how he constructs and links shots to follow lines of movement, sometimes disrupting the flow with shock edits, from wide shots to extreme close-ups, or destroying lines of action for shots of discontinuity, producing momentary disorientation for dramatic impact. The natural locations and geometrical features of the road, its vanishing points, the painted lines, the horizons, the telephone poles and fences produced a uniform, if sometimes beautiful and abstract, quality to the visuals and again helped produce a dynamic power.

David Eggby on the film's visuals:

> The visual style of the film came from early talks with George Miller and Byron Kennedy about low, wide lenses skimming the road and letting the format enhance the wasteland and highways, etc. – very Sergio Leone. The CinemaScope format was perfect. This was a different approach to action, it was a once in a lifetime chance to create something that hadn't been done before. It was very raw filmmaking. I don't remember the specific film stocks apart from the fastest was 100asa – not great when the Todd AO lenses were like T3.5 wide open and no money for a huge lighting package. We did, however, have a good tracking vehicle for its days which we could mount a jib arm on. As far as I am aware there wasn't anything done in post[production] for the look of the film. Remember, this was pre-CGI. I didn't even get to sit in on the grade.

Shooting in medium and close-ups can be a haphazard undertaking in widescreen, so Miller sought to get maximum punch and avoid dead space by providing compositional symmetry within the frame. This was paramount for single shots and 2-shots, (the types of shots which dominate the opening car chase), and the close-ups. Miller did not invent centre-framing, but it is an integral aesthetical feature of *Mad Max*. When cutting gets fast, the action and detail of the shot is never swamped by the frenetic nature of the montage or causes eye strain. Everything registers, it keeps the viewer orientated regarding spatial awareness and the director a paid great amount of attention when composing shots to consider eye-trace (where a person will look in any given shot). In recognising this, Miller's use of centre-framing and eye-trace awareness means he could focus the viewer's attention where he wished, cut shots rapidly and lose zero in terms of visual info, while maintaining rhythm, emotion and storytelling. Much was made of Miller's use of centre-framing in *Mad Max: Fury Road*, but the director had used it in his debut. In a 2015 interview with the Den of Geek website, journalist Brendon Connolly brought up Miller's use of centre-framing and visual fluidity, to which the director responded enthusiastically:

> With something moving so quickly, and with so much action, it can become like visual noise. Not disorienting but annoying, really. There has to be a strong causal relationship between one shot and the next. It's just like when you're composing music, there needs to be a real strong connection, in many ways, in the structure of the music. So central framing helps you to do this [in the visuals]. On the big, wide screen you can predict where the eye will be going a lot of the time.

But the choice to shoot in anamorphic widescreen presented its own issues. The Todd AO lenses caused persistent problems. Only one of them worked. Shooting outside and making use of the sky as a background canvas, the mixed weather created havoc with shot matching. Eggby explained: 'It is always hard to keep a visual continuity on a big exterior film and I'm sure if you scrutinised [the film] shot by shot it varies a lot, but when the action is working it doesn't matter.'

Mad Max Begins

Mad Max sets an ominous mood with Brian May's Bernard Hermann-style scoring arrangements. The unsettling quality of the score brings a frisson of the unexpected and establishes an almost bombastic energy. The director hired May after seeing 1978's Ozploitation classic, *Patrick*, a film about a young man with telekinetic powers. Miller enjoyed the score's distinct Hermann-esque qualities. The Hollywood composer became famous for themes which provided emotional moods set apart from the imagery and featured tonal experimentation. His method for big screen scoring was radical and set him apart from others in the industry at the time. The director believed something similar would be the perfect fit for his debut. In *Mad Max*, shrieking strings and pounding drums immediately suggest an aural sense of chaos, peril and doom.

There is a quirky detail present in the credits sequence, which slaps the names of creatives involved like it's in a rush to get through the traditional formality of titles. The use of '=' to denote each person's chief responsibility or function is unusual. Rarely (if ever before) has a credits sequence used 'Photography =' or 'Director ='.

Mad Max title card

Typically, credits roll with a standardised 'Produced by' or 'Directed by' or 'A film by'.

The title card design appears against a black background, whooshing in, looking like a customised hood ornament on the front grill of a car or truck. The alliterative power of the title '*Mad Max*' figuratively brands the audience. The title *Mad Max* was temporarily changed during post-production to 'Heavy Metal', when distributors Village Roadshow grew concerned '*Mad Max*' would be a tough sell, and 'Heavy Metal' was somehow more appropriate. After brief dillydallying, Kennedy Miller and Village Roadshow came to their senses and the film reverted to the original title.

The very first image we see in the *Mad Max* universe is the Halls of Justice, at dusk. The decrepit building is presented in a low-angled establishing shot. The place looks eerie, weeds cling to the signage and vines crawl over the walls. It is primarily a haunting, gothic image of decay and ruin, looking less like a cop shop, more Dracula's castle. It also recalls the opening of *Citizen Kane* (1941), with its depiction of Charles Foster Kane's grand estate, Xanadu. If not immediately obvious, the image of a building fallen into hard times is the first sign the future isn't to be a sunny upland.

A lap dissolve (Miller's preferred method of transitioning between spaces) takes us to a desolate road with car wreckage dotting the bottom of the frame. Telephone poles line up like a phalanx of soldiers stretching off into the distance, like an honour guard of the damned. It's also an image post-rainfall (rainy surfaces always look great on

Mad Max takes place in a decaying world where police stations look like gothic ruins.

film). The second shot perfectly establishes *Mad Max*'s dominant imagery and settings: roads, widescreen vistas, the horizon stretching into the distance. Text appears on the screen accompanied by the clattering keys of a typewriter: 'A few years from now...'

There is yet another dissolve to an upside-down skull and crossbones image (denoting danger or death). In three very quick shots, Miller establishes three major components: social decay, the violent threat of the road and a warning sign the film we are about to see is a 'candy lane of murder and mayhem,' to quote Robert Downey Jr's Aussie reporter, Wayne Gale, in *Natural Born Killers* (1994).

The next shot takes us to a new day and different location. The weather has changed (it's sunny). We are now in bucolic surroundings, yet the parched grass gives the environment a slightly barren look. A Main Force Patrol car sits idle and the road sign reads: 'Anarchie Road, 3km'. Shots 1-4 run a mere 10 seconds, but establish so much, from the locations to the widescreen framing and composition with big skies constantly looming, roads venturing off into the distance, the telephone poles, road signs and fence posts combining to form graphic and spatial unity. The eye of the viewer is always drawn to the centre of the frame, time and time again, showcasing Miller's composition preferences and making sure that even when he cranks up the montage to machinegun style, there is no straining to see, even when shots last a few frames.

As noted in Chapter 1, *Mad Max* is gleefully anti-authoritarian and the next sequence of shots, commencing with a rising crane rig movement, depicts a tubby copper named Roop staring down the sight of a rifle. Is he hunting? Has he nailed a perp? No. There is a cut to a couple having sex in an open field (living a bit dangerously, given the country's abundance of deadly snakes). We then share Roop's POV through the crosshair of the rifle. This un-heroic, un-policeman-like behaviour recalls the line in *Dirty Harry*, when his new Latino partner, Chico Gonzalez (Reni Santoni), asks jokingly if he got the sobriquet 'Dirty Harry' because he was a peeping Tom.

A medium-long shot introduces Roop's partner, Charlie (John Ley). He's chilling out with his feet sticking out of the car window (this MFP vehicle is codenamed 'Big Bopper'). A Ford Falcon XB sedan with a 302 V8 engine, in a previous life it was, like Max's initial MFP car, formerly owned by the Victoria police and refitted for the movie. Charlie gets a message through that there's a bit of action headed their way. 'We've got a cop killer,' March Hare (another MFP unit) tells Charlie. Whistling and honking the horn to attract Roop, the shot reverses back to Roop on the concrete block staring down the rifle's sight. There is an iris-type effect of the couple, before cutting back to Roop, who lets out a laugh. Following is yet another crosshair/iris effect, depicting the couple scarpering sharpish across the field. Cut to: Roop laughing then turning away from the field and getting down off the concrete block.

Just 12 individual shots in a mere 49 seconds of screen time establish the speed at which Miller not only stages actions but conveys information. The film really doesn't pussyfoot around.

The Chase

Upon setting up the start of the chase, we are introduced to Max Rockatansky. In contrast to Roop and Charlie, Max is composed, cool, level-headed and possesses nerves of steel. The shot opens in close-up on a road sign reading: 'HIGHWAY 9, SECTOR 6'. In lower case: 'high fatality road – deaths this year = 57'. Underneath this is 'Main Force Patrol' with the 'O' replaced with 'A', so it reads: 'Main Farce Patrol'. This bit of graffiti, twinned with Roop and Charlie being a pair of berks, demonstrates again the classic Aussie anti-authoritarian streak at work. As the camera pans left across the road from the fatalities sign, the shot opens into a landscape view and we get our first glimpse of Max (he's fixing or playing around with his car, the Yellow Interceptor (a Ford Falcon XB sedan with a 351 V8 engine, 1974 model)). Like Roop and Charlie, Max is possibly killing time out of sheer boredom. Miller, throughout the opening 12-minute chase sequence, teases the character's introduction proper, with clever use of disembodied close-ups, long shots or reflections in mirrors. Such use of shots helps create an aura, a mystique about the man who will emerge as an anti-hero figure. Max suits up ready for combat, each action he performs in the following shots appears ritualistic.

From a wide shot, we go in for a close-up on Max's hand, momentarily in frame, as he works on the car engine. On the radio, a woman's voice robotically serves a reminder about police conduct. Max then walks to the driver's seat, in medium close-up. These shots are teaser images, as Miller cuts back to Roop and Charlie who bicker like a couple of kids. Roop wants to drive but Charlie won't let him. The car exits and is followed by an interior medium shot of Roop answering the radio call to March Hare. 'Hey Sarse, what's the form on this thing?'

Miller returns to Max listening in over the radio. We only see his torso and the towel hanging over his right shoulder. Sarse tells Roop the villain they're chasing is a 'twisto bikie, a scoot jockey' (classic Mad Max colloquialisms). There is medium close-up showing the back of Max's head. He cleans his hands. Sarse delivers more info on the perp: 'A few hours ago he kills a cop down in Sun City and goes beserk.' As the dialogue continues, there is another cut and shot of Max walking (we see only his leather boots). We learn this demented bikie has escaped in an MFP Pursuit Special (a 1972 Holden HQ Monaro) and he's headed towards Big Bopper and Max.

Sarse and Scuttle (played by Stephen Clark and George Novak) are introduced (framed travelling left) as they drive after the creep-o we will soon learn is the Nightrider. Three points of action have been established and three different locations: Max, Big Bopper and March Hare. The Nightrider is referred to as a 'terminal psychotic' and, on that note, there is another cut to an interior, medium close-up 2 shot, travelling left, establishing the visual continuity and pursuit between Sarse and Scuttle and the Nightrider. The lunatic is introduced laughing his head off like a hyena. Travelling with him is a woman.

As the stolen Pursuit Special is being tailed by the March Hare, the shot is presented and framed from a very low angle, literally the camera has been placed on the road, with the smoke billowing from the March Hare and the Monaro zipping off toward the horizon. The Big Bopper screams into view off the horizon, travelling camera right, in what looks like discontinuity, following the previous shot with the Big Bopper, but it achieves an Eisenstein-like montage effect, whereupon there is an energy produced by a collision between two shots. What's more, it provides a unity and spatial grounding for the Bopper's own sense of direction, as it is now heading towards the March Hare and Pursuit Special. In roughly two minutes of screen time and thirty-plus shots, Miller and his editors have established three different locales, three lines of action, making use of parallel montage to construct a logistically complex chase scene. Miller did not give himself a break when setting down on paper his film's opener. It's worth reiterating, David Eggby shot the entire film on one camera with lenses which caused serious grief.

Max is again reintroduced zipping up his leather jacket (in medium close-up). Followed by another Max tease: attaching a gun holster to his torso. We then cut back to the Monaro travelling in a low-angled shot, then a closer shot of the loon screaming and hollering. The camera pans away to the March Hare and to an interior 2-shot of Sarse and Scuttle. 'We're about a half mile off Anarchie Road, you'll see him any minute now,' Sarse informs his colleagues.

By now, the Big Bopper has screeched off a country lane, is back onto the asphalt and heading screen left. Roop yells at Charlie, needling him about his driving. 'Rip the guts out of it!' The sequence continues: a close-up of Charlie looking uncertain, with Roop's dialogue carrying over into the next shot. He says: 'Give it the bejesus!' Roop preps his sawn-off shotgun, to take a pot shot at the Nightrider. This is the first instance of what is a *Mad Max* icon-prop: the sawn-off shotgun. It is at this juncture where Miller unifies the space between Big Bopper and March Hare, using reverse eyeline shots. 'See him yet?' March Hare asks. Roop responds, seeing the Monaro, in the reverse shot: 'Got it.'

As the Big Bopper closes in on Monaro, attempting to ride alongside so Roop can take his shot, Miller and his editors heighten the suspense by cutting back and forth between close-ups and wide shots. It becomes a tête-à-tête, two police cars chasing down a crook like hunting dogs. The side profile on the Nightrider staring towards the Big Bopper gives the distinct impression he's totally getting off on the threat posed to him by Roop's gun. His nihilistic bravado means he will literally stare death (the sawn-off shotgun) in the face and do so with pleasure. As a seasoned crim, the Nightrider is loving the chase and it is here, at this moment, he applies the brake, leading Big Bopper to overshoot and avoid what would have been a collision. Miller frames the shot of Big Bopper almost as if it's going to smash out of the screen and into the audience. Miller also finds time include a pun on the action we've just witnessed: a 'Give Way' sign spinning furiously around from the force of the air stream caused by the passing vehicles. Big Bopper spins its back end, as Charlie hits the brakes. The MFP vehicle crashes right into the sign (the shot lasts barely a frame). Out wide, Big Bopper looks totalled, the siren and bonnet have detached from the vehicle. They are down, but not out of the game just yet. Another interesting thing occurs here. One of the very few handheld shots in the entire film. The camera moves towards Charlie at the wheel, like a documentary crew are going in to survey the damage. Roop and Charlie answer Sarse, with the Nightrider's laughter carrying over into the shot via the radio. 'Keep going, keep going. We're okay,' Roop acknowledges.

Max has been absent from this bit of sequence, while it focused on the chase between Big Bopper, March Hare and Nightrider, but as Roop and Charlie are momentarily gathering their senses before recommencing pursuit, Rockatansky is reintroduced via a low-angle dolly shot siding up to Max's MFP vehicle. He puts on sunglasses. The lower part of his face is teasingly captured in the wing mirror. The Nightrider's rantings soundtrack the shot, heard on the radio, aurally unifying different spaces.

Miller places the camera almost at ground level, to achieve a dynamism between the shot, the cut and the composition.

A lull in the chase

As stated, Miller deploys lap dissolves to transition between locations and between key sequences. This is the general rule of thumb, not an overall stylistic diktat. After four minutes of ripping action and teasing introduction of the hero, the location and scene transitions to Fat Nancy's café and introduces another supporting player in the film's story: Jim Goose a.k.a. The Goose. Goose is Max's bestie and he rides a motorcycle (a 1977 Kawasaki KZ1000 with customised fairings).

The camera snakes down to the bumper of a vehicle and tracks across to Goose's bike. A radio dispatcher is calling him, but he's inside eating and conversing with an acquaintance about an accident he once witnessed (detailed in Chapter Two). After putting the bloke off his dinner, comically asking 'What's the matter?', Goose picks up the guy's plate and proceeds to pile it on top of his own. It's hard not think Miller is making another anti-authoritarian gag here: a greedy pig.

An elderly gentleman notices the high-speed pursuit between the Monaro and the March Hare. 'Cor, look at that!' The cars blaze by and the patrons of Fat Nancy's all take notice. Goose realises he'd better scarper and join in the pursuit, puts down his plate on the counter and rushes out. *Mad Max* writer, James McCausland, is the guy behind the counter and he has a single line of dialogue: 'Catch ya later, Goose.'

Jim runs to his bike, theatrically rolls over the bonnet of a parked car (another satiric stab at cop-movie clichés). A tow truck pulls out of the car park, no doubt sensing the opportunity to make a bit of money from scrap metal.

The chase gets bigger

Once Goose and the tow trucks have left the car park at Fat Nancy's, Miller establishes one of the recurring set-pieces of the franchise: the big chase involving multiple vehicles. Miller would revise this core set-piece again and again throughout the mythology. Whereas *Mad Max 2* and *Mad Max Beyond Thunderdome* culminated in epic chases, *Mad Max* begins with one, front-ending what is typically a denouement, reversing tradition and attempting to captivate the audience from the get-go.

A low-angle close-up of the Monaro's front is accompanied by the Nightrider's yelling. This use of a jump cut not only cranks up the bedlam up a notch, it provides a shock: the car looms before us. The car moves to the right of the frame and the MFP vehicles come into view. Goose's bike enters frame left, the camera tracking from a low angle (road level). Meanwhile, Max is listening in still to the on-going pursuit and he hasn't yet made his move. There is yet another disembodied side profile shot, focused on his sunglasses. Max glances left, as if acknowledging the audience, the bridge of the sunglasses centre-framed and the road reflected off them. It looks cool. Max *is* cool. While the others are furious and flustered, Max hasn't yet turned mad, he's Cool Max.

The countryside setting of the chase so far transforms when Goose rides over a bridge (coming from screen right and into a town-like setting). Again, to get maximum impact from the framing and composition, Miller uses a crane to lift the camera. Whereas the rubber road was used as a duel between cops and crims, the story shifts to an urbanised space and with urbanised spaces come people. The Hitchcock factor becomes evident with the introduction of a young mum with a pram. She crosses a road. Next, a camper van comes into view the camera, panning right as the ute and caravan enters frame left. Sirens blare. Miller, here, is setting up one of the film's major stunts: a set-piece involving the Big Bopper crashing into the caravan. The woman, the child and the ute are like pieces on a chessboard. The camera continues to pan into a landscape shot with roadworks and a British-style red phone box (used in Victoria at the time, though edged out since). The woman with the pram meets a bloke and they bicker about a guy named Jonathan. This mundane domestic argument might be the most realistic bit of drama in the entire *Mad Max* canon. It is hilariously ordinary compared to where the series goes, though the argument serves as a bit of dramatic distraction as the toddler climbs out of his pram, while the ute performs a U-turn and stops in the middle of the road. The toddler runs into the road and falls over. It is not out of the realms of possibility that this shot/action is a foreshadowing of Sprog's death, later in the film, where he is mowed down by Toecutter's gang while clutched in his mother's arms.

To further the sense of action, drama, expectation and suspense, Miller follows with a low-angle close-up of the Monaro's grill and the snarling engine. Again, the camera pulls out into a wide shot, with the MFP closing in behind. There is a jump cut to a wider low-angle setup, depicting the Monaro and the MFP vehicles rounding a bend. Then it's a shot of a camper van leaving a storage centre at speed. (For years, a story went around that this was Miller's own Mazda sacrificed for the movie, but the director doesn't remember it that way.) Charlie reacts to the imminent crash. He ducks out of frame. The money shot! Metal on metal! A terrific spectacle of glorious automobile carnage: the Big Bopper careens into the Mazda, followed by a jump cut to the Mazda pirouetting post-collision. March Hare drives past the wreck of the Mazda, which is still spinning, and the Big Bopper, now pulled up to the side of the road, faces the other direction entirely. Sarse and Scuttle look back through the rear window to survey the devastation. Once again, Big Bopper has come a cropper, Roop and Charlie find themselves humiliated, though they're still not out of the race. Roop, in a side-profile shot, is victorious at having started the engine. There is a reverse angle shot from the back of Big Bopper. 'Pursuit' is emblazoned on the boot – an ironic comment on the fact their car has been totalled, but they're doggedly continuing. Sirens blare and the car shrieks off, smoke billowing from the vehicle's backend.

Having been embarrassed by the Nightrider and stopped by a hapless driver, Roop is by now royally pissed off. 'I'm gonna have him!' the MFP officer declares. Back to the Monaro, low angle, centre frame, as the car manoeuvres away, revealing March Hare tailgating the Nightrider. The camera moves out. This close-up into a panning wide shot is a stylistic device used several times by Miller, as it conveys not only visual information (reiterating spatial awareness) but provides a crucial sense of flow and movement. Cut to: Sarse sticking his head out of the March Hare, yelling at folk to stay off the road. It's an amusing moment, the only instance of cops policing the public and acting with concern for their safety.

As Big Bopper doggedly ploughs on, the camera pans left to reveal Goose's bike not far behind. There is then a jump cut to Goose on his bike, then a cut to the toddler running up the road, then a cut to the Monaro on the left of the frame, the March Hare on the right. A close-up is then deployed on Marmaduke (the floozy to Nightrider's skag). She looks worried the Nightrider is about to kill a kid. The sense of peril and the prospect of infanticide is heightened by a reverse shot from inside the Monaro looking out through the windshield at the little boy. Miller cuts to a close-up of the Nightrider grinning. It is this kind of blackly comic setup which would have a strong reaction from conservative critics of the film. Is the director really going to give us a scene of a psycho relishing the prospect of mowing down a child? Well, yes, but it occurs later in the unfolding drama.

In medium shot, the little boy notices the cars approach and the next image is a wide shot of the Monaro and March Hare occupying both lanes, hurting along the blacktop. There is the rare use of a crash-zoom, a technique prevalent and abused in 1970s cinema, on the ute driver noticing the approaching vehicles. The scenario is about to reach its zenith, as the arguing couple notice the toddler has vanished and the cars pass between the kid on the road. The subsequent close-up of the mother screaming perhaps references the mother's cry in Eisenstein's *Battleship Potemkin* (1925). It is a reaction shot as shock jump cut. Miller, here, creates a sense of elastic time, by slowing down the frame rate as the mother's face screams, producing a frisson of horror. The images playing at slow motion is dictated by the action and the culmination of shots. Cut too fast and the shot doesn't work. It's both pragmatic and logical to slow things down just a notch. It might well also be influenced by Miller's time as a doctor. He would have been well used to seeing people exploding with emotion at unwelcome news or seeing something horrible.

With the shot of a red telephone box and an upturned MFP vehicle next to the caravan in the distance, we're presented with what they call a 'goof', or a continuity error. The image captures March Hare before it has upturned and crashed. For it has been established Big Bopper is behind March Hare, so it cannot be Roop and Charlie, and we have seen no other MFP vehicle join in the chase or crash. The appearance of a British-style red telephone box is intriguing, too. As we know from Australian cinema's past and the New Wave boom, filmmakers fired satirical and political shots at white Australia's mother country. Smashing up the phone box can be read as another satirical swipe, though it could easily just be a telephone box getting obliterated as a prop. These red phone boxes were a feature in Victoria state from the 1950s until they were phased out in the 1980s.

Further points of action

Another money shot occurs in this pedal-to-the-metal sequence along the urbanised thoroughfare, when the Big Bopper crashes into – and through – the caravan which has halted in the middle of the road. This set-piece is the film's major bit of spectacle. For it to have maximum visual impact, the image is slowed down, so the audience can take in the beauty of the flying debris. It is another moment where Miller creates elastic time. If music is visual rock 'n' roll, as the director says, these slow-motion moments are akin perhaps to a crunching power chord reverberating.

Goose arrives on the scene and loses control of the bike. As it slides along the ground, Miller cuts to the bloke in the ute, whose caravan has just been spectacularly totalled. He ducks, as if expecting to die. Instead, as a bit of counter action to the big smash, Goose's bike gently slides into the driver's side door, barely making a tap. The scene then cuts away to the Big Bopper slowing down in a field. Again, the image is played in slow motion, providing a bridge between Goose's gentle glide into the ute and the Big Bopper now out of the game for good. In the next shot, the red telephone box lurches over and smashes to the ground.

Having survived the scrape, Goose is in a strangely jovial mood, responding to the ute driver's query about what just happened with: 'I dunno know, man. I just got here meself.' The Big Bopper is now toast. The exposed bonnet is partially draped with a lace curtain and we see another rare instance of the handheld shot, which pans across to Charlie clutching his bloodied throat. Roop radios in, informing his fellow MFP team, that Big Bopper is done. 'You better send a meat truck. Charlie's copped a saucepan in the throat.'

As Goose radios Max, we are treated to another of Miller's teasing-the-hero shots that have dotted the sequence. We see a close-up on Max's sunglasses. 'We are 100 percent snafued,' Goose tells his friend. Max asks Goose if he's okay. The scene cuts back to Goose, who replies with a typically sunny and upbeat: 'Nothing a year in the tropics wouldn't fix.'

Tow trucks then arrive on the scene. The tow trucks are important as they help to establish the scavenger theme on which the sequels are built. The Nightrider's dialogue is now heard and continues into the next 6 shots. The dialogue is among the most famous lines in the entire *Mad Max* canon. 'You should see the damage, bronze. Metal damage, brain damage. Are you listening, bronze? I am the Nightrider. I'm a fuel-injected suicide machine. I am a rocker, I am a roller, I am an out-of-controller. I'm the Nightrider, baby!' The villain's dialogue is a play on and mimicking of lines from AC/DC's track, Rocker: 'I'm a rocker, I'm a roller, I'm a right out-of-controller.'

Now that Big Bopper, March Hare and Goose are out of the race to defeat the Nightrider, it's time for Max to enter the fray. Miller continues to tease Max in close-up: Max shifting the gear stick followed by a close-up on the tail pipe which then opens out into a wide shot and pans right as Max drives off to meet the escaped maniac somewhere on the road.

The Nightrider continues his ranting: 'The Toecutter! He knows who I am! I am the Nightrider! I am the chosen one! The mighty hand of vengeance!' In a road-level landscape shot of a grassy bank and the blacktop stretching away into the distance, Max's Yellow Interceptor appears from screen left and applies the brakes. Another shot in this short sequence again features Max's sunglasses, this time reflecting the landscape, followed by a close-up on Max's gloves. 'I'm hotter than a rollin' dice! Step right up, chum, and watch the kid lay down the rubber road right to freedom,' the Nightrider blabs.

As discussed, the car replaces the gun in the world of Mad Max as the totem of masculinity and lethality. As Max waits for the appearance of the Monaro, we hear the Interceptor growl. It's a curious use of sound, not just showcasing the engine power of the cop car, but one akin to the western's cowboy's hand hovering over his pistol as he's ready to draw. The Yellow Interceptor versus the stolen Pursuit Special now becomes a duel and a reworking of the classic confrontation between the lawman and the bandit in western movies.

The Nightrider is now at the point where his fiery rhetoric and taunting must face reality. Things get serious. He sees Max's vehicle and senses a life and death skirmish is on the cards. He pushes Marmaduke away from him. Miller emphasises this extraordinary opening sequence is coming to a close, using close-ups of the police sirens whirling on Max's car, a low-angle side profile on the Yellow Interceptor screeching away and shot-reverse-shot between Max and the Nightrider as they head towards each other, neither intending on backing out of a fight. As the two cars are within touching distance, Miller uses an extreme close-up and zoom-in (another rare use of this camera lens movement) on the Nightrider's face and eyes. The close-ups not only focus attention on the extreme emotion felt by the Nightrider, but they provide a sense of the unescapable. There is a close-up on the Nightrider screaming, a POV shot of him gripping the steering wheel and making a hard turn to avoid a smash and a wide shot of the cars passing each other on the road, as they travel in opposite directions. Max has won the duel. The Nightrider has been defeated in this ritualistic display of macho posturing, and he cries like a little kid. Max has spun the car and is in direct pursuit. He honks his car horn, tauntingly, and tailgates the Monaro. The Nightrider has lost his kill-thrill mojo completely. Max's Yellow Interceptor grinds the rear bumper of the Monaro. As the cars speed along, Nightrider morose and with nothing to prove now his masculinity has been questioned and his demented bluster revealed as exactly that, the maniac fails to notice a workman with a red flag attempting to get his attention. The Nightrider makes an abrupt turn narrowly missing a truck carrying oil drums. The Nightrider loses control of the car and it begins to swerve violently. We are at the scene of a road accident, an irony appearing: the vestiges of a smash are about to cause another. The extreme close-up on the Nightrider's bulging eyes is another famous shot from the movie, but the use of the close-up and then opening wide into a smash and explosion provides the sequence's finale with a fiery end.

Now that the Nightrider has gone up in flames, we are finally introduced to Max proper. The shot recalls John Wayne's introduction as the Ringo Kid in John Ford's *Stagecoach* (1939). Max is out of the Yellow Interceptor looking at the Monaro. As with the Ringo Kid's intro, the composition is heightened by use of the dolly shot. Here, the wide shot moves into medium shot from a low angle. Max has arrived.

Max surveying the devastation of the explosion.

CHAPTER FOUR: BEYOND ANARCHIE ROAD

Into the Wasteland: *Mad Max 2*

It is a truth universally acknowledged, that a hit movie must be in want of a sequel. Talk of a *Mad Max* follow-up was almost immediate, with Byron Kennedy asked about a second film in the July 1979 TV Week article (quoted in Chapter Two). He didn't rule it out completely. Wounded Max had driven off into the rainy night, his wife, child, and best mate all dead, but their demise had been avenged. This open-ended conclusion, Rockatansky heading off to destinations unknown, made the character's return plausible. Kennedy, however, mentioned several other projects he and Miller had cooking on the stove (these projects, it would soon turn out, were put on the backburner). Though Kennedy readily conceded, in the age of *The Godfather: Part II* (1974), *Jaws 2* (1978) and *Rocky II* (1979), sequels were big money spinners and audience appetite for more meant the odds looked good for Max's return.

Exhausted after *Mad Max*'s chaotic shoot and intense post-production, Miller wasn't so keen. His favourite topic of conversation at the time was every single fault he found in his debut. In the past, the director has joked that the cutting in *Mad Max* was so quick as he had to cover up the countless mistakes. These flaws obsessed him. What he'd imagined in his head, Miller believed, was not captured on camera or up there on the big screen. But a sequel, arguably, would serve as a corrective, the chance to have another stab, to do things better. An evening stroll with friend and screenwriter Terry Hayes, around the suburb of Hastings and Westernport Bay (now infamous for being the home of serial killer Ashley Coulston, who gunned down three students in a house in Burwell, east Melbourne in 1992), changed Miller's mind, and the seed of an idea was planted by the sight of a chemical refinery.

The central premise of *Mad Max 2* was inspired by the chemical plant location, while the sequel would also take place after an apocalyptic event. The refinery on an isthmus at Westernport Bay inspired the oil compound in the desert in *Mad Max 2*. Social tensions over the scarcity of fuel at petrol stations across the country became a savage fight to the death for control of what natural resources remained. Primarily, this was the 'guzzaline' (the film's colloquial term for gasoline). After the civilised world has collapsed and survivors reduced to scavenging and pillaging, folk were more than willing to kill for a tank of juice. Darwin's survival of the fittest became Miller's survival of the maddest.

Mad Max 2 was released Christmas Eve 1981 in Australia (with worldwide releases following in 1982). The sequel was even more ambitious in scope. Armed with a far greater budget (circa AU$4 million), it made $100 million worldwide. *Mad Max 2*, unlike its predecessor, was a gigantic hit in the US. Roger Ebert called *Mad Max 2* a film of 'pure action, of kinetic energy organized around the barest possible bones of a plot'. Writing in 2005, for The Independent, sci-fi author JG Ballard anointed it with the highest accolade imaginable: Punk's Sistine Chapel, adding: '*Mad Max 2* is by far the best of the *Mad Max* series. With its insane vehicles and fearful body-armour, it is a vision of Armageddon as autogeddon.' The Sistine Chapel comparison was also made earlier by Phillip Adams, who described Mad Max as 'a sort of blood-stained Sistine ceiling for the '70s'. (1979: 41).

Today, *Mad Max 2* is rightly acknowledged as a masterwork and one of the greatest genre movies of all time. It further established George Miller as a singular filmmaker and master craftsman, and of course he was able to refine his concept of 'visual rock 'n' roll' cinema. He did this by cutting back the dialogue to a bare minimum, letting the images, montage and sound effects take over. There is a visual purity to *Mad Max 2* going back to the days of the silents. Gibson utters about 16 lines in the whole film, instead letting his charismatic screen presence do the talking. In comparison, the original Max is a chatterbox.

The *Mad Max 2* version of the character is a continuation of a man who has lost everything, but he now boasts added mythic resonance. Max has become a wanderer of the wasteland, a feral scavenger attempting to outrun his demons in a world of constant threat and terror. There are two goals in this post-apocalyptic hellscape: acquiring 'guzzaline' for the black-on-black V8, and living another day. If *Mad Max* was set in a world on the brink of destruction, the sequel confirmed the future belonged to the hoon. The hoonmageddon had occurred.

Urban and rustic landscapes with undulating green grass hills gave way to the starker, ancient, primal Outback. Filming took place around Silverton, Broken Hill and the Mundi Mundi plain (all in a remote part of north west New South Wales). This time, too, preparation work was done to ensure a fast turnaround and fewer on-set problems during filming. In other words, Kennedy and Miller learned from their mistakes and were intent on not repeating them ever again. The shoot commenced during the Australian winter of 1981 (May) and, like *Mad Max*, the sequel is effectively another spin on the western genre, though this time tapping more directly into Joseph Campbell's hero monomyth, detailed in *The Hero with a Thousand Faces* (1949). Max had to die symbolically to be reborn.

Miller connected the two films via a black-and-white opening montage reel of stock footage cut with scenes from *Mad Max*. Newsreel footage detailed the collapse of civilisation, showing images from WW2 and other barbaric sights. Miller shot a new scene of Max by the graveside of his wife and child, appearing in his old MFP uniform and walking with a crutch (this shot is in colour). It looks like an outtake from the first film, but it isn't. Miller and cinematographer Dean Semler shot it to bridge the narratives, to show Max's backstory as part of the flashback device at the start of the sequel (those who had not seen the first film would soon get the gist of Max's story). In wide shot, with smoke billowing, Max walks away from the graves of Jess and Sprog. A further link is drawn between the end of *Mad Max* and the sequel by repeating the exterior wide shot of Max driving at night in the rain, which dissolves into an establishing shot of a new landscape.

Max by the graveside of his deceased wife and child in Mad Max 2

The film's narrative is concentrated around Max Rockatansky needing fuel for his battered V8. A chance encounter with a scavenger (Bruce Spence's Gyro Captain) leads our hero to an oil refinery in the desert. The people who live at the refinery have been targeted by Lord Humungus and his tribe of miscreants, who want control over the oil and stage regular assaults against the compound and its residents. The compound leader, known as Papagallo (Michael Preston), has a plan to escape by driving north to reach a land of sunshine and promise seen on a tatty old postcard in the group's possession. It does seem a tad peculiar that some of the oldies, who are way older than Max, are childlike in their belief the road north leads to safety. Max knows the place no longer exists, but he agrees to drive a tanker full of fuel through a route blocked by Lord Humungus.

Bloodied, bruised and royally conned, Max is left with zilch at the film's end. Wearing a wry smile on his face, the ending of *Mad Max 2* is one of the most bitterly ironic in screen history. Max helps save the compound and gets the remaining group to safety by playing the patsy. Max got screwed over. The truck, supposedly carrying the guzzaline, is filled with nothing but red sand. A nondescript school bus was carrying the precious cargo, but Lord Humungus doesn't notice, nor does Max. Nevertheless, the road warrior is venerated by the survivors as their savour and so transformed into a mythic being, a noble fighter in a terrible world.

In Mad Max 2, Max Rockatansky is a road warrior surviving day by day, the antihero cop is transformed into a mythic figure.

Goodbye, Soldier: *Thunderdome* and the End of a Trilogy

The summer and autumn of 1985 saw the widespread release of *Mad Max Beyond Thunderdome* and the conclusion of what for thirty years was a trilogy. Pre-production on the film, though, was marked by the cruellest tragedy. On Sunday 17 July 1983, a Bell Jetranger helicopter owned and piloted by Byron Kennedy lost power in the air and crashed into Lake Burragorange, south of Sydney. Kennedy was severely injured in the crash and subsequently died from his wounds, having spent the night in freezing waters. He was 33 years old.

A maverick talent taken far too soon, his fine legacy lives on today in the ever-popular *Mad Max* franchise and the several landmark television mini-series he and Miller produced in the early 1980s. The Australian Academy of Film and Television Arts Awards recognised Kennedy's gigantic contribution to his homeland's film industry by naming an award in his honour. It is given out every year to winners who, like Kennedy, showcase 'outstanding creative enterprise within the film and television industries... whose work embodies the qualities of Byron Kennedy: innovation, vision and the relentless pursuit of excellence.'

George Miller roped in co-director George Ogilvie to take command of dialogue scenes, while he focused exclusively on action set-pieces and stunts. Ogilvie was brought in due to his experience working with actors. He had been a theatre director and teacher before venturing into television and cinema. Importantly, Ogilvie had previously directed Mel Gibson in Arthur Miller's *The Death of a Salesman*, for the Sydney stage, and the two Georges previously collaborated on the mini-series *The Dismissal* and *Bodyline*, the latter the story of the 1932 Ashes cricket contest between Australia and England.

Beyond Thunderdome is the *Mad Max* franchise at its most commercially orientated and soft-edged. An accusation levelled at the original was explicit in the third outing: Max had gone Hollywood. The series' snarling punk attitude and nihilism was turned into something more palatable for American viewership. It now had an MTV look and music-video sheen. Max was a Christ-like redeemer facing off against Tina Turner's Aunty Entity, the ruler of a hellhole called Bartertown.

The film's desert locales and American blockbuster scope was inspired by David Lean's *Lawrence of Arabia* (1962). Miller went so far as to hire Maurice Jarre to compose the musical score, while Tina Turner provided a hit single in 'We Don't Need Another Hero' (Miller directed the music video, with Turner standing under a spotlight on a platform, and clips from the film were incorporated into the promo). Jarre's score is very different from Brian May's Bernard Hermann-style horror-tinged, strings-heavy compositions. The theme song became a standard in Turner's concert repertoire. At some point before release, Jarre's original overture-style theme was replaced by the Turner ditty, 'One of the Living'. In fairness, the switch works far better with the credits, tying as it does in song Max's status as the perennial reluctant hero figure. Turner warbles 'Don't want to fight but sometimes you've got to.'

In the years since its release, *Beyond Thunderdome* is generally considered the least successful iteration of *Mad Max* and therefore the runt of the litter. It was favourably received in 1985... with caveats. Gene Siskel, writing for the Chicago Tribune, liked the film overall but noted *Beyond Thunderdome* becomes preachy, before continuing in a more positive note: '...before we and Max are bored, director Miller returns Max to his roots, a screaming chase sequence through a desertlike Australian landscape.' Siskel's long-time cohort, Roger Ebert, wrote a glowing review, today featured on the late critic's website (rogerebert.com), calling it the best of the bunch and praised the concept of Thunderdome most of all:

> Thunderdome is the first really original movie idea about how to stage a fight since we got the first karate movies. The "dome" is a giant upside-down framework bowl. The spectators scurry up the sides of the bowl, and look down on the fighters. But the combatants are not limited to fighting on the floor of the arena. They are placed on harnesses on long elastic straps so that they can leap from top to bottom and from side to side with great lethal bounds. Thunderdome is to fighting as 3-D chess is to a flat board. And the weapons available to the fighters are hung from the inside of the dome: cleavers, broadaxes, sledgehammers, the inevitable chainsaw.

Australian film critic Alexandra Heller-Nicholas is a fan of the movie, though, like others, with certain reservations. In an episode of the Plato Cave radio show (18 May

2015) devoted to the *Mad Max* series, she discusses the film's weaknesses: 'Even as a defender, the middle section of this film does dip, and it is a bit wobbly. It almost feels like a failed Terry Gilliam film, in places.'

The Influence of *Mad Max*

Mad Max's cultural credentials are evident in the array of films, television shows, music videos and art installations it influenced, or on works which make direct reference to it. An early one is 1985's *Top Gun*, directed by Tony Scott. Best friend to Tom Cruise's Pete 'Maverick' Mitchell is Anthony Edward's Nick 'Goose' Bradshaw. Like *Mad Max*'s Goose, *Top Gun*'s Goose dies mid-way through the film and his demise deeply affects the lead. The link goes no further, but as a nod to *Mad Max*, it's a strong one.

James Wan and Leigh Whannell's *Saw* (2004) was partly inspired by the infamously brutal scene in *Mad Max*, where the rogue cop comes across Toecutter goon, Johnny the Boy, and then forces him at gunpoint to tie himself to an auto wreck leaking petrol. Max gives Johnny the Boy a choice between sawing off his ankle, giving him a chance to escape an imminent fiery blaze, or just waiting to go up in flames. Wan and Whannell have stated that this pivotal scene, where Max's scheme of vengeance is completed, though leaving him burnt out and with no friends or family, influenced them massively, when they were penning their breakout horror film. It was a box office smash which, along with Eli Roth's Hostel series, kickstarted the 'torture porn' boom in horror.

The Quentin Tarantino-scripted *True Romance* (1993) included Christian Slater's Clarence Wurley bemoaning the Oscars and the mediocre movies that win Academy awards. '*Mad Max*, now that's a movie!' he exclaims to Hollywood producer, Lee Donowitz (Saul Rubinek). QT delivered further homage in *Death Proof* (2007). As well as thanking George Miller in the end credits, cinema's great magpie paid homage to the Nightrider's bulging- eyes-popping-out-of-their-sockets, during the climatic chase between Stuntman Mike (Kurt Russell) and the ladies in the Dodge Challenger. The finale of *Death Proof* runs like a bravura combination of all the director's favourite muscle car movies: from *Mad Max* to *Vanishing Point* (1971) to *Gone in Sixty Seconds* and *Dirty Mary, Crazy Larry* (1974). Tarantino does not ape Miller's montage, but the intention behind the cap-doffing is obvious enough as a general homage to an era when car chases and car crashes were done for real. 'CGI has fully ruined car crashes. When you watched them in the 1970s, it was real cars, real metal, real blast,' the director explained in the *Grindhouse* (2007) book, released to accompany his and Robert Rodriguez's joint film venture in B-movie nostalgia.

The Netflix pop cult phenomenon, *Stranger Things*, threw in a reference in Season 2. Maxine Mayfield (Sadie Sink) uses the video gamer tag 'MADMAX' at the arcade where she hangs out, while Australian art duo, Soda_Jerk, incorporated scenes from the entire *Mad Max* franchise into their controversial video essay, *Terror Nullius*, a 55-minute art piece remixing Australian pop culture items to examine the country's 'contemporary moment'. The Irish Times (March 2019) described the medium length film as 'White Australian mythology pummelled on screen'. The Australian Centre for the Moving Image, which coughed up AU$100,000 to fund the film, ended up backing away from public support, as some in the Australian media deemed the resulting work as 'un-Australian'. Another body, the Ian Potter Moving Images Commission, also withdrew its support in promoting a work they'd partially funded.

Panos Cosmato's *Mandy* (2018), stars Nicolas Cage on a rampage of revenge, after a cult leader and his goons murder his wife (played by Andrea Riseborough). The film's trippy aesthetic is a world away from George Miller's montage collision of sound and image, but its leather-clad troubled hero avenging his missus, biker gang baddies and wacky villain who isn't the norm, echoes *Mad Max*. Even more recently, Kleber Mendonça Filho and Juliano Dornelles' *Bacarau*, which premiered at Cannes in 2019 and shared the Best Screenplay prize with Ladj Ly's *Les Misérables*, is set in near-future Brazil, where a small town community is besieged by American tourists who have paid off a corrupt local mayor to hunt them down. While having no direct link aesthetically or narratively with *Mad Max* (*Bacarau* is closer to an acid western), Filho and Dornelles took the idea of setting their film just a little bit into the future, in order to give the material a distinct sci-fi dystopia flavour and to craft a nightmare vision of a country currently under the rule of far-right populist, Jair Bolsonaro.

Mad Max Remixed: *Terror Nullius*

Commissioned by the Australian Centre for the Moving Image, video essay *Terror Nullius* (2018) became a political hot potato. Ingeniously put together by Soda_Jerk (Dan and Dominique Angeloro), the video essay is described on the art duo's website as 'Part political satire, eco-horror and road movie. *Terror Nullius* is a political revenge fable which offers an unwriting of Australian national mythologies. Binding together a documentary impulse with the bent plotlines of Australian film texts, Soda_Jerk's revisionist history opens a wilful narrative space where cinema fictions and historical facts permeate each other in new ways. The apocalyptic desert camps of *Mad Max 2* become the site of refugee detention, flesh-eating sheep are recast as anti-colonial insurgents and a feminist motorcycle gang gets medieval on Mel Gibson's ass and smashes up the Interceptor.

This playful video essay uses footage from *Mad Max* to satirise Mel Gibson and denounce his misogynistic, racist rants. As the duo told the author via email, 'We're giant fans of Miller, just not Gibson'. Footage from *Mad Max* is incorporated in a brilliantly comic sequence, which starts by picking up on the feminist credentials of *Mad Max: Fury Road* and uses it to spring off into a female-led vigilante attack against Gibson, mixing in audio from the released tape recordings of the star verbally attacking his partner, Oksana Grigorieva. The vigilante attack begins with the shot seen in the film of Max fixing his car (the camera pans from a road sign across to the Interceptor). The music playing over the scene is lifted from Paolo Sorrentino's *The Young Pope* (2016), drawing a comic link between the perils of Catholicism and Gibson's notorious beliefs in a traditional form of the religion. On the rear end bumper, Soda_Jerk have digitally added a 'Catholic to the Max' bumper sticker.

When Max switches on his radio, instead of the police operator detailing the on-going pursuit between March Hare and Nightrider, we hear a cricket match. Soda_Jerk cut in a scene from Brian Trenchard-Smith's *Turkey Shoot* (1982) – the woman in the grass carrying a crossbow. Max waiting for the Toecutter gang is spliced with the woman with the crossbow. She fires and Max falls to the ground (the editing making it look as if she's hit him, whereas in the film it's Bubba Zanetti who has shot Max). Soda_Jerk then cut to Imperatior Furiosa driving, with Alanis Morrisette's

'You Oughta Know' playing. In the backseat is Holly Hunter's character from *Top of the Lake* Season 2 and beside Furiosa is Kate Winslet in *Hideous Kinky* (1998). Max is then run over by the Toecutter gang, as in the film, but the crafty editing makes it look like a girl gang is heaping vengeance on Gibson. Nicole Kidman in *BMX Bandits* (1983) rides over his body, Michelle Pfeiffer in *Grease 2* (1982) appears, Kidman as Virginia Woolf in *The Hours* (2002) looks on, smoking a cigarette, the girls from *The Sapphires* (2012) appear too (the inclusion of First Australians a pointed comment perhaps on their near total absence in the series). The scene concludes with Toecutter's gang smashing up the Yellow Interceptor, though mixing in shots of women with baseball bats (including Claudia Karvan in *Jack Irish*, Soda_Jerk selecting the actor because she plays an artist who makes art from wrecked cars). The way in which Soda_Jerk change the meaning of the shots in *Mad Max*, to invoke scenes of Gibson being terrorised, is brilliantly Kuleshovian in effect, both *Mad Max* and *Terror Nullius* being directly inspired by Russian montage binds them in an unexpected way. The Interceptor is bashed in and 'We Are Not Things' is spray-painted in green on the twisted wreckage. Teenaged Nicole Kidman reappears in footage from *BMX Bandits* to jump over the car. The Interceptor is then set on fire, as Muriel Heslop and Rhonda, from *Muriel's Wedding* (1994), look on and laugh. The Toecutter's gang ride off.

Terror Nullius got into all sorts of trouble with conservative thinkers when shown at art galleries in Australia, in 2018. Not only that, the funding bodies who backed it distanced themselves from the finished product. It was described as 'un-Australian' and 'controversial', but Soda_Jerk's barnstorming recontextualization of New Wave Australian cinema and its classic movies again shares with *Mad Max* a distinct, quintessential and humorous anti-authoritarian stance. *Mad Max* caused a kerfuffle upon release and so too did *Terror Nullius*. The artists were not poking fun at Miller's movie, but reshaping shots and sequences to critique their country's toxic masculinity and targeting Gibson for mockery.

Mad Max and *The Rover*

Based on a short story co-written by actor Joel Edgerton, *The Rover* was originally set to premiere at the 67th Cannes Film Festival (2014) in the 'Midnight Screenings' strand, typically reserved for genre movies, before it was rescheduled to a more prestigious late evening gala screening slot. A lot of hype surrounded its appearance at the world's number one movie festival, partly due to its perceived relation to *Mad Max*. But for director David Michôd, this spiritual connection threatened to become a millstone around the neck of what is a poetic and dark existentialist tale. Michôd went to repeated lengths in interviews, to make sure expectations were tempered and dialled down a notch or two.

Eric (Guy Pearce) is a farmer and ex-soldier stopping for a beer in a small hamlet, somewhere in the Outback (filming took place in South Australia, north of Adelaide, coincidentally where many exterior scenes for *Mad Max Beyond Thunderdome* were shot). A band of robbers crash their vehicle and steal Eric's. A grizzled and short-tempered fella, he pursues them along the highway, only stopping when he's knocked out cold during a confrontation. Back in town, he meets dim-witted Rey (Robert Pattinson), one of the thieves left for dead during a shootout. When Eric learns of the connection, he kidnaps him and forces the idiot to help track down the rest of the group so he can retrieve his car, a fixation which at first seems very strange until the final shots of the movie explain why he was so intent on getting his wheels back. Inside the boot of the car was a dead dog, a poignant symbol of Eric's nostalgia for his old life and literally the last bit of it the crooks took from him. At the end, not unlike Max Rockatansky, the character has accepted he has nothing left to cling on to and his old life is dead.

The *Mad Max* comparisons largely stem from the fact Edgerton and Michôd set their story in the future and situated it around a great shift in the country's fortunes. And, as with *Mad Max*, the future is stripped down and desolate, hinting at rather than showing social decay. Instead of opening with 'A few years from now…' *The Rover* begins with the capitalised legend: 'AUSTRALIA. TEN YEARS AFTER THE COLLAPSE.'

The Rover is an uncompromising and moody work, one beautifully shot in searing dusty ochre colours by cinematographer Natasha Braier. The narrative pacing is deliberately slow, key information is held back from the audience in a bid to keep a sense of mystery and uncertainty, and while there are bursts of action – car chases and gunfights – it's basically *Mad Max* reimagined as an arthouse movie (eagle-eyed viewers will note Scoot McNairy's character in an early scene brandishes a sawn-off shotgun at Eric), wherein a lone hero loses the last vestiges of his humanity. The film is littered with fatalistic dialogue, such as Eric's suggestion to Rey, that 'You should never stop thinking about the life you've taken. That's the price you pay for taking it.' However, one cannot imagine Max pondering the implications of wiping out Toecutter's gang, for more than a few seconds.

In *The Rover*, Australia is in crisis, yes, but it's nothing to do with a forthcoming apocalypse. *The Rover* is about the social strain that a realistic and crushing economic crash could have on the country. Known as 'The Collapse', it had to be extreme enough for the mining industry to be owned entirely by foreign companies and for the vet played by Susan Prior to bring up the fact people are eating dogs. In one scene, Eric mentions how he murdered his wife and her lover, and nobody came to arrest him. There is no Main Force Patrol in the world of *The Rover*, only mercenaries guarding mining interests. In the Outback, the law has let criminals run rampant. In another scene with a mercenary, state capital Sydney is disparaged in a way that makes it sound like the place has turned into a Bartertown-like hellhole.

Michôd, in a 2014 online interview conducted by this author for the defunct Grolsch Film Works, described the world of his film:

> The world of the movie is the world of a western economic collapse. In a way, it's also the world of a profound geopolitical shift. It's one of the reasons why it felt very specific to the Australian desert, this film. You get little indicators, here and there, that there's still a functioning mining industry and it is feeding China and feeding Chinese mining interests. There are people in this world still making money and making a lot of it.

The director also mentioned the similarities to *Mad Max*, really trying to distance his movie from George Miller's film, but the comparisons are often too prominent to ignore. 'From that very first day when Joel Edgerton and I started talking about the possibility of this movie, we knew we were potentially trespassing on George Miller's property. That is the power of *Mad Max* films.'

Rockatansky Returns

On 7 May 2015, *Mad Max: Fury Road* held its first screening at the iconic Chinese Theatre, in Hollywood. The director, his cast and original Max, Mel Gibson, were in attendance. A week later, on 14 May, the film had its international premiere at the 68th Festival de Cannes (screening Out of Competition). In an age where youngsters may not know *Mad Max* from Pepsi Max, its box office appeal was far from certain, Miller and Warner's hoping the nostalgia factor and the character's place in cinema history would bring in the money. Warner Bros. ploughed over $200 million into its production and advertising budget. In order to make sure baby boomers, 1980s kids and millennials remembered or understood the series, a 'legacy' trailer, featuring clips from the original trilogy, was put out onto the internet.

Was Miller's series about to experience a franchise recharge or would it prove a nostalgic trip too far? *Beyond Thunderdome* had seen a decrease in ticket sales in Australia, suggesting the buzz was wearing off even back then, the character in danger of maxing out his cultural credit. There had been reports of a troubled shoot in Namibia, and word began to go around the production was in difficulties with its stars, Tom Hardy and Charlize Theron, at loggerheads and barely talking to each other. Reshoots were undertaken in Australia long after filming officially wrapped. While this is an industry standard, sometimes when transferred to media stories, it gets turned into a negative message along the lines of 'the film is going to be a dud, folks'.

Mad Max: Fury Road began when Miller took a flight from LA to Sydney, sometime in the 1990s. The director, letting his mind wander, dreamt up a story (a group of women fleeing a terrible man). This scenario was a *Mad Max* adventure waiting to happen, Miller decided. Gibson was ready and willing to put on the leathers once more, but as production stalled and stalled, Miller's attention turned to other projects, the troubled star eventually declined to appear. To borrow a famous line from the *Lethal Weapon* series, the original Max was too old for this shit.

British actor Tom Hardy was recast in the role and Charlize Theron signed up to play a new character, Imperator Furiosa, a War Rig driver with a mechanical hand. Furiosa in many ways took on the old character's most recognisable attributes and characteristics: the silent stares, the haunted look, only speaking when necessary.

Max, in comparison, and arguably for the first time, deserves the moniker 'mad'. It's an eccentric performance from Hardy, rendering the hero a gibbering wreck with a constantly changing accent, one which goes all around the world from the Aussie overheard in the intro 'My name is Max. My world is fire and blood,' to what sounds like West Country English in lines such as 'How much more can they take from me? They got my blood, now it's my car!'

Filmed in Namibia, South Africa and studios back in Sydney, after the original selected location (Broken Hill) was deemed unsuitable due to unseasonal rains turning arid desert into an oasis of flowers, the director pretty much reinvented the action movie wheel and put other blockbusters to shame. In the age of CGI, where films look like computer games and the action on screen feels weightless, Miller again decided to shoot the stunts for real and augment the visuals with computer-enhanced effects. As mentioned, the physicality of the stunt work and organised chaos imagery is what gives *Mad Max* movies their special movie magic. Miller did not lose track of this aesthetic truth in the age where it's easier to use green screen and fill in the blanks later. Doing things for real provides the *Mad Max* movies with their wow factor.

If the fourth entry's Australian-ness was muted to a large degree, still Miller found a way for his latest *Mad Max* adventure to echo with Aussie audiences. *Mad Max* expressed or reflected on hoon culture, whereas *Mad Max: Fury Road* picked up on the fad for 'chroming', the colloquial term for toxic gas inhalant abuse, which can cause seizures, heart problems, breathing issues and in some cases even death. It is prevalent among First Australians and teenagers. This socially conscious inspiration point connects *Mad Max to Fury Road*, Miller once again implementing homegrown concerns about public health into his sci-fi extravaganzas.

Many people wished to know, in the run up to the release, where in the *Mad Max* timeline the new one fitted. Max lost the black-on-black in the sequel, he didn't have it at all in *Beyond Thunderdome*, but it turned up again in *Fury Road* and is soon trashed and transformed by Immortan Joe's War Boys into a hybrid beast (Miller again reflecting on an Aussie car culture). Max is angry as hell when he notices what's happened to his motor (those with big love for the black-on-black will no doubt share Max's distress). But the car's inclusion demonstrates that Miller was never interested in presenting a strict chronology. Every film in the series was a reinvention, remake, reboot, reimagining, and all the other buzzwords associated with properties Hollywood likes to use when attempting to dress up old material in new duds. Sam Raimi achieved a similar effect by remaking *The Evil Dead* (1981) as *Evil Dead II* (1987), not really paying too much attention to continuity.

After the public sat down to watch it, a section of online fanboys raged. They were miffed at what they saw as Max being relegated to the role of sidekick. It's a profound misreading of the character dynamics and storyline. Max isn't a sidekick or second wheel, he's an ally to Imperator Furiosa. Max in the sequels is never the catalyst for events. He is a wanderer, always playing the reluctant hero. In the sequels, Max is told about the compound full of oil by Bruce Spence's Gyro Captain. He comes across Bartertown presumably by chance, having had his vehicle and camels stolen. In *Fury Road*, he is kidnapped by a party of War Boys. Each time, he makes a key decision to act the hero. Pure vengeance fuels his retaliation in *Mad Max*, in *Fury Road* Max has revised his stance to 'retaliate first'. He says this to Furiosa, when the Bullet Farmer is hot on the War Rig's tail.

In her award-winning essay, 'Furious and Furiosa', for The Overland literary journal, Alexandra Heller-Nicholas noted Miller's radical new take on the character and the story's focus on the emancipation of women from patriarchal terror. Max is not the great and *only* hope; Furiosa is equally a warrior and champion. Max became an ally, not a sidekick. 'In *Mad Max: Fury Road*, normative masculinity is not just broken, it is literally diseased,' writes Heller-Nicholas. Furiosa's ascension is achieved by the overthrowing of Immortan Joe's tyranny. Max being Max, the ultimate loner, he departs at the end, declining to join the new order, but not before he and Furiosa exchange a look, one that communicates respect and comradeship. Their friendship is confirmed in a single line, as Max attempts to save a wounded and dying Furiosa, by an emergency blood transfusion, an act furthering the sense these two soldiers must rely on each other to stay alive. 'My name is Max,' he softly tells her, having previously refusing to divulge any personal information.

Miller did not plan to be so political and progressive, but he recognised the power of the story as he and his co-writers developed the scenario. The director also drafted in activist and playwright Eve Ensler, who scored major success with *The Vagina Monologues*, for a week to workshop with the 'Brides', discussing all the themes the film throws up. Heller-Nicholas puts it that *Mad Max: Fury Road* is 'An important reminder that feminism is not about a simplistic men vs women configuration, but rather a battle on a unified front against systemic oppression based on hatred, ignorance and difference.'

Almost immediately from the film's release and for a year or two after, the talk of sequels regularly cropped up and occasionally Miller would confirm there were plans to commence with what he called *Mad Max: The Wasteland* or a spin-off involving Furiosa. Both Hardy and Theron signed on the dotted line for multiple movies, but in the age of Hollywood franchises ruling schedules, that's nothing remarkable or particularly noteworthy. *Mad Max: Fury Road* performed well overall, but nowhere near the same league standings as blockbusters zooming past the $1 billion mark. It made its production budget back, earning $154 million from 3,722 screens in the USA (according to Box Office Mojo website). It brought in a further $224 million from international markets, with $11 million of that coming from Australia. In the UK, it earned $27 million. The grand total is $378 million dollars. Not bad, but certainly not big-league blockbuster territory. As of writing, the prospect of these sequels being made have been snafued by Kennedy Miller issuing a lawsuit against Warner Bros. over unpaid earnings.

To tie-in with the blockbuster movie, as is studio practice in the age of synergy, a video game was developed by Avalanche Studios (based in Stockholm, Sweden) and released through Warner Bros. Interactive Entertainment, in September 2015. Max, voiced by Ben Foster, making him an unofficial third Max Rockatansky, longs to disappear to the Plains of Silence (the place referenced in *Fury Road*). After a run-in with Scabarous Scrotus, a son of Immortan Joe, he must head to Gastown (its shimmering towers spied briefly from afar in *Fury Road*) and retrieve the famous black-on-black, while ridding the area of War Boys and various villains. The game received mixed reviews, but design-wise it fit aesthetically with Miller's blistered depiction of the Wasteland and works as a prequel to events in *Fury Road*.

In 2016, *Mad Max: Fury Road* won 6 Oscars from 10 nominations, taking: Best

Production Design, Best Film Editing, Best Costume Design, Best Makeup and Hair Styling and Best Sound Editing. Miller and his team swept up awards at the AACTA Awards in December 2015, these accolades from home and abroad indicative of the fact that while Max might be local hero, he was now also a worldwide success.

Conclusion

Mad Max is a benchmark in Australia's cinema, even if initially the film might have been overshadowed by *The Road Warrior*, and its influence best embodies the post-apocalyptic subgenre. Today, leather-clad Max is an Australian icon alongside Skippy, the Pilbara Wanderer, Ned Kelly, Dame Edna, Crocodile Dundee and Muriel Heslop (what an Avengers-style team that would make).

Mad Max represents pure guerrilla moviemaking. It is this humble quality, mixed with an audacity somewhere between inspired and crazy, that makes *Mad Max* a true one-off; the type of thing you can only get away with once. George Miller did not singlehandedly invent the post-apocalyptic actioner, but like George A. Romero's acclaimed zombie feasts, his specific iteration of the planet going down in flames provided a template for others to follow. The 'lone warrior in a broken world' actioner wouldn't have evolved without the seed planted by the original. Throughout the 1980s and into the 1990s, especially, Italian genre flicks, Ozploitation titles and Hollywood tried to rework the *Mad Max* formula. They were pale imitations.

BIBLIOGRAPHY

Age, The (1984), Green Guide, Victoria

Australian Associated Press (1979)

Adams, P (1979), *The Dangerous Pornography of Death*, The Bulletin, Sydney, Australian Consolidated Press

Adams, P in Murray, S (ed.) (1980), *The New Australian Cinema*, London, Elm Tree Books

Adams, P (2015) The Australian, New South Wales, News Corp Australia

Aitken, S (2017), *David Stratton: A Cinematic Life*, Sydney, Stranger Than Fiction Films, Running time: 97 mins

Alberge, D (1983), *Films and Filming*, Croydon, Brevet Publishing Ltd

Andersen, T (2003), *Los Angeles Plays Itself*, Thom Andersen Productions Running time: 169 mins

Ballard, JG (2005) The Independent, London, Independent Print Ltd

Bastién, AJ (2017) Vulture, New York magazine, New York, New York Media, LLC

BBFC (1979 & 1992) *Mad Max* censor board notes, London

Bennett, Colin (1979), The Australian, New South Wales, News Corp Australia

Brite, P (1996) *Screen Violence* edited by French, K, London, Bloomsbury

Brady, Tara (2019) The Irish Times, Dublin, Irish Times Trust

Buckmaster, L (2017), *Miller and Max: George Miller and the Making of a Film Legend*, Melbourne, Hardie Grant Books

Chute, David (1982), *Film Comment*, Vol 18, July-August issue, NYC

Connolly, K (1981), *Australia's Pride is its New Wave Films*, NY Times, NYC, The New York Times Company

Corliss, R (1980), *Time*, NYC, Time Inc.

Cousins, M (2004) *The Story of Film*. London, BCA

DuBose, M (1979), *Sydney Morning Herald*, Herald and Weekly Times Ltd

Ebert, R (1985) *Mad Max Beyond Thunderdome* review

Eggby, D (2016) Interview with author

Hanrahan, J (1979) The Sun, Sydney, Fairfax Holdings Ltd

Hall, K in Murray, S (ed.) (1980) *The New Australian Cinema*, London, Elm Tree Books

Hallam, L (2017) 'Nature Found Them Guilty: Revenge in Australian Exploitation Cinema' Miskatonic University lecture, London

Hitchcock, A in *Hitchcock* (1966), Truffaut, François, London, Simon and Schuster

Heller-Nicholas, A (2015) Overland Journal, Victoria University, Victoria

Kennedy, B & Miller, G quoted in Beilby, P & Murray, S (1979), Cinema Papers, Melbourne, Cinema Papers Party Ltd

Kuleshov, L in Cinema: *A Critical Dictionary*, Vol 2: Kinugasa to Zanussi, edited by Richard Roud, London, Martin Secker and Warburg Limited

Malcolm, D (1979), The Guardian, London, Guardian Media Group

Martin, A (2003) *Australian Screen Classics: The Mad Max Movies.* Sydney, Currency Press

McCausland, J (2006) *Courier-Mail*, Brisbane, News Corp

McDonald, M (1979) The Courier-Mail, Brisbane, News Corp

McDonagh, M (2004) The Postman review, Film Journal http://www.filmjournal.com/postman

Miller, G (2008) Australian Screen interview: https://aso.gov.au/people/George_Miller_1/interview/

Murray, S (1980) *The New Australian Cinema*, London, Elm Tree Books

Pike, A in Murray, S (ed.) (1980), *The New Australian Cinema*, London, Elm Tree Books

Rohdie, S (2006) Montage, Manchester, University of Manchester Press

Scott, S (1979) *The Telegraph*

Siskel, G (1985), Chicago Tribune, Chicago, Tribune Media Services

Smith-Trenchard, B (2018), Interview with the author

Tarantino, Q (2007), *Grindhouse: The Sleazed-Filled Saga of an Exploitation Double Feature*, New York, Hachette Book Group

White, B (1979), *The Mirror*, Sydney, News Corp

Whittaker, T & Wright S (2016), Locating the Voice in Film, University of Oxford Press, Oxford

CONSTELLATIONS

'This stunning, sharp series of books fills a real need for authoritative, compact studies of key science fiction films. ...the volumes in the **Constellations** series promise to set the standard for SF film studies in the 21st century.'
Wheeler Winston Dixon, Ryan Professor of Film Studies, University of Nebraska

www.ingramcontent.com/pod-product-compliance
Ingram Content Group UK Ltd.
Pitfield, Milton Keynes, MK11 3LW, UK
UKHW030801150425
457405UK00006B/73